Helping
Children
Cope

Helping
Children
Cope

JOAN FASSLER

Illustrations by
William B. Hogan

AN AUTHORS GUILD BACKINPRINT.COM EDITION

AN AUTHORS GUILD BACKINPRINT.COM EDITION

Published by iUniverse.com, Inc.

For information address:
iUniverse.com, Inc.
5220 S 16th, Ste. 200
Lincoln, NE 68512
www.iuniverse.com

Originally published by The Free Press

ISBN: 0-595-16720-9

Printed in the United States of America

Contents

PREFACE   ix

ACKNOWLEDGMENTS   xiii

Chapter I: Death   **1**

Stories About Nature and Change   3
Stories About the Death of Pets or Loss of Other Objects   3
Stories That Might Relate Well to Issues Surrounding Human
    Death   9
    *Stories Showing Warm Relationships Between Elderly
      Individuals and Young Children* 9
    *Stories That Raise the Issue of Possible Death in the Near
      Future* 9
    Stories Centering Around the Actual Death of a Person 11
    *Stories About Children Who Have Experienced the Death or
      Loss of an Important Individual in Their Lives Sometime in
      the Past* 16
Information-Type Books About Death   17
When a Child Dies   20
    Books About the Death (or Threatened Death) of a Child 20
    Stories About Death Among Anthropomorphized Animals 21
Conclusion   22
References   22
Juvenile Bibliography: Books That Might Help Young Children
    Talk About or Share Some Feelings Concerning Death   23

Chapter II: Separation Experiences   26

Reassuring Stories To Help Counteract Fears of Abandonment   28
Bedtime Stories   29
   Gentle Stories To Help Relax a Child at Bedtime 29
   Stories Portraying Some Inner Concerns and Anxieties
    Surrounding Bedtime 31
   Stories About Dreams and Dreaming 33
Separation-Type Stories That Might Relate Well to Early School
   Experiences   34
Separation from Parents for Reasons Not Related to School
   Activities   39
Accidental Separation from a Parent or Parent-Figure   40
Separation from a Well-Liked and Trusted Individual (Friend,
   Teacher, Therapist, etc.)   42
Separation Feelings and Children's Books: Some Further
   Suggestions   44
Conclusion   47
References   47
Juvenile Bibliography: Books Relating to Early Childhood
   Separating Experiences   48

Chapter III: Hospitalization and Illness   51

Imaginative Stories That Portray Hospital Experiences   52
Information-Type Books About Hospitalization   57
Books Portraying Experiences and Emotions That May Have
   Special Meaning for the Hospitalized Child   62
   Separation Feelings and the Hospitalized Child 63
   Nighttime in the Hospital 64
   Self-Esteem and the Hospitalized Child 65
   Maintaining a Sense of Independence and Autonomy 67
   Encouraging an Open, Honest Expression of Feelings 68
Books To Help Build Personal Courage   73
Books Describing a Visit to a Doctor's or Dentist's Office   74
Stories About Illness or Pain in General   78
Conclusion   79
References   79
Juvenile Bibliography: Books To Help Children Cope with
   Hospitalization and Illness   80

Chapter IV: Lifestyle Changes   86

The New Baby   87
Moving to a New Home   93

Adoption 100
Divorce 114
References 127
Juvenile Bibliography: Books Relating to Selected Lifestyle Changes 129

Chapter V: Other Potentially Stress-Producing Situations

135

Financial Stress 136
Changes in Parents' Working Arrangements 138
Changes in Family Constellation 139
When a Parent Goes to Prison 142
Fire, Floods, Storms, and Other Emergency Situations 148
References 152
Juvenile Bibliography: Coping with Other Potentially Stress-
Producing Situations 153

INDEX OF JUVENILE BOOK AUTHORS AND TITLES 156

GENERAL INDEX 160

Preface

AS FAR BACK as I can remember, I have felt an affinity for children's literature: a delight in the whispered message of a story and the secret significance it may reveal. For the past five years I have been sharing this delight with professionals interested in child health and have noted again and again how often and naturally these two paths cross—how an understanding of child development and a knowledge of children's literature can be skillfully interwoven to bring children and books together in a highly personal and provocative manner. During this time I have collected considerable information about the use of books and stories to help children grow. Individuals working with young children, such as psychologists, psychiatrists, social workers, pediatricians, nurses, primary-school and nursery-school teachers, day-care personnel, and librarians, repeatedly inform me that this information has helped them create highly successful story–child–adult interaction experiences—experiences that initiate communication, reduce anxieties, enhance development, and encourage growth. The purpose of this book is to share such information with a wider audience—to bring to the attention of individuals interested in child health selected information from the vast field of children's literature that may carry a special meaning to them in their work with young children.

This publication concentrates on certain areas of potential stress, such as hospitalization, illness, death, separation experiences, moving, adoption, divorce, birth of a baby in the family, and other situations that may strain a child's coping skills. Each chapter presents an initial discussion of professional viewpoints concerning the topic under consideration, followed by a discussion of selected children's books that may help children gain mastery of the situation. Many of the books discussed have been used at the Yale University Child Study Center and nearby hospitals and schools. Often, questions to help initiate discussion are suggested in relation to specific children's books. Other techniques that have been found successful in using books and stories to help children face difficult situations are also described. Difficulties with certain books, as well as serious areas of neglect in the children's book field, are noted as well. Each chapter concludes with a list of professional references concerning the chapter topic, or topics, followed by separate listings of recommended juvenile books.

The emphasis here is on books for children in the four-to-eight-year age range. Where an adequate selection of such books is not available, books for older children are sometimes discussed with the suggestion that these be adapted for use, where appropriate, with younger children or be viewed as an inspiration for the creation of new books on similar themes for the younger child.

This book, of course, does not touch upon all areas of stress; nor does it consider all potentially valuable children's books. It draws instead on the extensive experience I have had in using and recommending books for young children for specific purposes and concentrates on those books and those situations that have, to date, brought considerable feedback from colleagues in various health-related disciplines (e.g., pediatrics, psychiatry, psychology, education, social work, nursing, etc.) regarding the effectiveness of specific experiences with children and books. Hopefully, however, the material will be sufficiently tantalizing to encourage readers to extend the principles proposed here to new juvenile publications and other potentially stress-producing situations.

This publication has been planned, therefore, as a reference guide, presenting information not easily accessible to individuals who work with young children and wish to assist children in coping with various kinds of stress. The suggestions offered are in no way intended to negate the joy of children's books or to detract from their importance as a literary or artistic medium. The intent, rather, is to focus attention on another, equally important, aspect of the children's book world; to encourage individuals concerned with healthy child development to consider books as possibly valuable communicative-aids; and to help interested, caring adults recognize, more readily, the potential for growth that may exist in a shared story experience.

JOAN FASSLER
Child Study Center
Yale University
New Haven, Connecticut

Acknowledgments

I WISH TO EXPRESS my sincere appreciation to the Grant Foundation, whose generous financial support to the Child Development and Children's Literature Program at the Yale Child Study Center made this book possible. In particular I wish to acknowledge the support, encouragement, and excellent counsel received from Philip Sapir, President of the Foundation, throughout this project. I also wish to thank Albert J. Solnit, M.D., Director, Yale Child Study Center, for his support and guidance in all aspects of this work. His keen insights into childhood and his sincere concern for the mental health and well-being of children have furnished inspiration for this work, as indeed they have for numerous people and projects in the past.

Other colleagues at the Child Study Center were instrumental in making this book possible. Ann Casper, Asa Flake, Richard Granger, M.D., Marjorie Janis, Kathryn Lustman, Sally Provence, M.D., Kyle Pruett, M.D., and Lois Wolf all shared valuable insights with me concerning children and books. I am sincerely grateful for their thoughtful suggestions and warm friendship over the past several years. For secretarial assistance I wish to thank Patricia Caddoo, Anna Clater, Myrtle McLean, Mary Migliore, and Florence Shapiro, each of whom contributed practical, innovative suggestions as well as excellent skills and rewarding friendship. Administrative talents contributed by Terry Przygocki and Ruth Parker of the Child Study Center, and research assistance contributed by Christina Jackson (presently at Notre Dame University) also are gratefully acknowledged.

Interest and information about children and books were generously offered by Dorothy Garey, Professor of Library Science, Southern Connecticut State College. Ruth Abrams, Rita Norman, and Sara Battison also provided valuable library assistance at different stages of this work. To each of these individuals I extend sincere appreciation.

David Biesel, my Editor at Macmillan, was a delight to work with throughout this project. I particularly compliment Dave for his foresight in seeing this material as a potentially valuable resource guide for a wide range of individuals interested in child health. George Rowland, my Editing Supervisor at Macmillan, contributed his excellent knowledge of English, suggesting changes in language and style with the utmost skill and sensitivity.

In addition to the Grant Foundation, other foundations have contributed support to various aspects of this work. Gifts received from the Morton Foundation (New York, New York) and the George A. Long and Grace L. Long Foundation (Hartford, Connecticut) are gratefully acknowledged.

Finally, I wish to thank my husband, Leonard Fassler, and our children, David and Ellen, for their assistance in innumerable ways in making this project not only possible but also pleasurable.

To the staff of the Yale Child Study Center, to numerous juvenile book authors and artists whose work has emotionally touched the lives of young children, to teachers, parents, students and hospital personnel who volunteered to read and discuss stories with young children, and to the many children who participated in such story sessions, I also extend a sincere thank you.

It has been a pleasure to be involved with children and books during the past several years. It is a privilege now to be able to present here some of the insights and information this work has generated.

Death

IN DISCUSSING THE FIELD of juvenile books, a recent publication suggests that books for young children should, above all else, speak such truths that they will help to put young readers in closer contact with their own inner selves (Lanes, 1971). Similarly, Simon Lesser (1957), in his classic publication, *Fiction and the Unconscious,* notes that one of the most important responses to literature is an emotional response. "We may be sure," Lesser comments, "whenever a reading experience is successful, intrapsychic harmony [on the part of the reader] is furthered to some extent" (p. 290).

If, in fact, we believe that children's literature can help children grow, it seems sensible, and possibly essential, to explore the field of juvenile books from a child-development as well as an aesthetic point of view, paying careful attention to the possibilities for emotional interaction between a particular child and a particular story (or storyteller). With this view in mind, members of various child health and health-related professions may be interested in considering juvenile literature as a potentially valuable communicative-aid.

The present chapter will focus attention on the topic of death as an example of stressful or anxiety-producing situation that may arise in early childhood. A number of books for young children that portray the death of storybook characters, or relate to some of the many emotional issues surrounding death, will be discussed. In each case, emphasis will be placed on the use of the juvenile books described as springboards for discussion between children and adults and on their possible value as an additional means of helping young children cope with experiences involving death.

There is, at the present time, a considerable amount of professional literature available concerning children's reactions to death (Bowlby and Parkes, 1970; Furman, 1970; Grollman, 1967; Kliman, 1968; Nagera, 1970). It has, for example, been suggested that when faced with the death of someone important in their lives, children are likely to go through an initial period of disbelief or denial; later, a bereaved child may spend considerable time remembering and discussing numerous experiences that he or she once shared with the deceased. There may be ambivalent feelings expressed here, such as anger that the dead person has abandoned the young child. There may also be guilt feelings, based, for example, on the belief that some misbehavior or momentary wish on the part of the child may have caused the death itself. Discussing these feelings with an understanding adult can play an essential role in the important healing process often referred to as grief-work. Eventually, if the mourning process is a healthy one, the child will begin to look for, and develop, substitute relationships in an attempt to fill the tremendous need that the death of a close person is likely to create in his or her life.

In all of this, one of the most supportive and helpful things an adult can do on behalf of a child who is coping with death is to encourage an open discussion and expression of feelings. The child must be helped to understand that the topic of death is not taboo and that his or her own fears and fantasies surrounding death can be explored from time to time with understanding adults.

Selected children's stories have proven helpful in initiating and encouraging such discussions. A limited number of books for preschool and primary-grade children concerning death are now available. Some juvenile publications deal with the death of pets; some deal sensitively with the death of human beings; others deal with the broad concept of death in general.

The use of such books, and the discussions they provoke, can, I believe, be beneficial long before a child is confronted with a situation involving death as well as after a child has experienced the loss of a loved one. "It is a clinical impression," notes John Schowalter (personal communication, June, 1974), "that children who are exposed to death in a non-frightening way, either through religion, the death of a pet or a not-too-close relative, tend to be more open and less fearful about death than those without this exposure." Perhaps carefully selected children's books and the discussions they initiate can become an additional and potentially valuable way to offer children such exposure.

Stories About Nature and Change

For preschool and primary-grade children, the topic of death can be approached, at first, by books dealing with nature and change. *The Growing Story,* by Ruth Krauss, shows how each animal, flower, and child grows and changes in its own special way. *The Bear Who Saw the Spring,* by Karla Kuskin, *Time of Wonder,* by Robert McCloskey, and *White Snow, Bright Snow,* by Alvin Tresselt, all portray changes, too. *Time of Wonder* illustrates the changing seasons, from spring to fall, as well as changes relating to the beginning and end of a storm. *White Snow, Bright Snow* and *The Bear Who Saw the Spring* both concentrate on the change from winter to spring, with each book emphasizing the beauty and the wonder inherent in nature. Such books encourage the belief that there is a time and a place for everything. They can be used to initiate discussion about the various cycles of life and may help children begin to understand that all living things, animals and humans, do eventually grow old and die. They can also lead into discussions highlighting the fact that death is an inevitable phenomenon, that it is part of nature's plan, and that its reality need not be denied or hidden.

Stories About the Death of Pets or Loss of Other Objects

Other books portray the death of pets or illustrate the reactions of young children to the discovery of a dead animal. *The Dead Bird,* by Margaret Wise Brown, a classic and well-loved children's story, is a beautiful example. In this story, some children find a dead bird and decide to bury it in a quiet spot in the woods. The children note that the bird is cold and dead, with no heartbeat at all. They agree that it will never fly again. Funeral rites are carefully planned. First, the bird is wrapped in grapevine leaves, and covered with sweet ferns and yellow flowers. The children sing a special song and create a small marking stone. And they cry because their singing is so beautiful and the bird is dead. Then every day, until they forget, the children return to the burial site to sing their song and put fresh flowers on the grave. The last illustration in *The Dead Bird* shows the children busy at play, once again, suggesting that by now they must have fulfilled a need to

acknowledge their encounter with death in an appropriate manner and, therefore, are ready to move on to other things.

In response to this story, children may want to share experiences and feelings concerning the death of their own pets- or other animals. Some may describe funeral procedures and rituals they may have created in the past for a dead pet. Comments that the bird is cold and dead and cannot fly any more often initiate discussion concerning the finality of death: young children frequently inquire if the bird in the story will still be dead tomorrow.

Interestingly, some reviewers have commented that the funeral rites in *The Dead Bird* are too elaborate for a bird. Similar opinions have been expressed from to time in adult discussions of this book. Apparently there are many individuals who adamantly believe that the death of a bird does not or should not merit such detailed attention. It is, however, likely that the children in this story *did* require an opportunity to acknowledge their own sadness and concern at meeting death. The rituals described here were created to help the children, not the bird. Real-life children with similar needs, who wish to conduct their own funeral ceremonies to commemorate the death of a pet or even a stray animal, should, I believe, be permitted and perhaps encouraged to do so.

In *The Tenth Good Thing About Barney,* by Judith Viorst, a little boy mourns the death of his cat. When Barney, the cat, dies, the young boy plans a funeral for his pet. The boy's mother suggests that he thinks of ten good things about Barney to tell his friends at the funeral. When the ceremony takes place, the little boy can recall only nine. Later, after helping his father plant some seeds, he thinks of a tenth accolade. "Barney is in the ground and he is helping to grow flowers."

There is an open expression of feeling in this story: a boy who cries deeply, acknowledges his sadness, and sincerely misses his cat. There are also understanding and sympathetic parents. And there is, additionally, a healthy affirmation of the ongoing nature of life, as the cat's death is portrayed in juxtaposition to the planting of seeds and the patient wait for new flowers.

Perhaps one cautionary note is needed here. The stress on ten "good things" about Barney might encourage overidealization of the deceased. Therefore, a discussion of this story should include the suggestion that there are often negative as well as positive memories to recall about a loved pet or person who has died, and that such memories, too, can be talked about and shared.

In *Growing Time,* by Sandol Warburg, a much-loved collie named King dies, and a small boy named Jamie mourns for his pet. King was very old; he had been part of Jamie's family for a long, long time. The adults in the family try to comfort Jamie, each in his or her own way. Uncle John tells him that death involves going back to the earth which is our home, while Grandmother assures him that King's spirit will never die; it will always live on in Jamie's heart because of the many memories stored there.

Several psychologically sound points are raised in *Growing Time,* points that might be sensitively woven into a follow-up story discussion. For example, an open expression of feelings is strongly encouraged here. Tears spill down Jamie's face, and he freely admits his great sadness and his longing for his dog. At one point in the story, Jamie states that he is almost *angry* at King for "going away," thereby verbalizing a reaction to death that may be frequently experienced, but seldom acknowledged. In addition, the fact that Jamie is not blamed in any way for his dog's death can be noted and discussed. Jamie did nothing to cause King's death; in fact, he gave King good and loving care. Still King died. Death simply occurs. It is not a retribution for any wrongdoing or evil thought on the part of a child. Finally, the story clearly indicates that King cannot return and play with Jamie again. He can return only in Jamie's heart and in his memories. This last point offers an excellent opportunity for children and adults to consider together some clear and honest statements concerning the realism and finality of death.

In addition to the death of pets, the destruction or loss of other meaningful objects has also been sensitively portrayed in children's literature. *The Red Balloon,* by Albert Lamorisse, tells the story of Pascal, a lonely French boy who has no sisters or brothers, no apparent friends, and a mother who does not allow him to keep any pets in the house. Pascal becomes deeply attached to a red balloon. As the balloon takes on more and more lifelike properties, an almost magical relationship develops between the boy and this much-loved object. The balloon accompanies Pascal wherever he goes, and together they take part in many exciting adventures.

Certain child readers (or story listeners) quickly grasp the importance of the relationship Pascal has created between himself and the red balloon, and they are indeed saddened when a group of cruel and taunting boys throw rocks at the balloon and finally destroy it. When the author subsequently notes that Pascal is "crying over his dead balloon," many young children accept this statement in a literal manner. For them, the balloon has indeed died. Perhaps because the young are still struggling to understand which things are truly alive and which things are not, they may be more likely to relate the destruction of Pascal's balloon to an actual death than would an older, more experienced child. In any event, *The Red Balloon* can help initiate discussion with young children about loss and death, not only in regard to inanimate objects but also in regard to people and pets.

The relation between *The Red Balloon* and death was first brought to my attention by a young mother whose husband had died in Vietnam. While studying children's literature in a graduate course at the University of New Hampshire, this mother read several stories to her four-year-old son, carefully noting his reactions to each story. The child became particularly absorbed in *The Red Balloon,* listening to the story again and again and examining the photographs with much attention. As they read about the balloon's destruction by a gang of cruel boys, the mother noted that her son, on one occasion, commented, "Just like daddy, just like daddy." The boy then began to ask several questions about his father's death, a topic he had previously been most reluctant to talk about. Apparently, something in Pascal's story motivated this child to talk about the sad and tragic death of his father. It is legitimate to question, however, whether the child discussed here was responding to the story itself, to his mother's reaction to the story, or, possibly, to some unique combination of story and mother. Some time ago, Martha Wolfenstein (1947) clearly demonstrated that the attitudes (conscious and unconscious) of a storyteller or storyreader greatly affect the manner in which a particular story is presented to a young child and, at the same time, affect the child's reaction to, and understanding of, the story itself. Perhaps, in the incident related above, the mother's own reaction to *The Red Balloon* was, in some way, passed along to her child.

This reminds us that each story-child-adult interaction is likely to be unique. Surely, no one story can be considered a panacea for all children who must face a stressful situation; nor can it be expected that a selected story will hold the same significance or elicit similar reactions wherever and whenever it is presented.

Not all books concerning death portray the topic in an honest and psychologically sound manner. Juvenile books about death, therefore, cannot *all* be considered helpful for a child coping with an actual death experience. For example, a small, wordless picture book entitled *A Boy, a Dog, a Frog and a Friend,*[1] by Mercer and Marianna

---

[1] Mayer, Mercer and Marianna. *A Boy, a Dog, a Frog and a Friend.* New York: Dial Press, 1971.

Mayer, is concerned, in part, with the death of a turtle. In this story, a sad little boy is busy digging a grave in order to bury a dead turtle, when suddenly there is a dramatic change and the once-dead turtle flips over and returns to life! Soon afterward, the resurrected turtle gaily trots off, following the boy, the dog, and the frog—the turtle being the fourth and newly found friend for this engaging group. Meanwhile, the interrupted burial procedures and, in fact, the whole topic of death are both cheerfully obliterated.

Children coping with death often have great difficulty accepting the finality of the situation. There is, therefore, little potential value, from a psychological point of view, to be gained by offering such children stories that emphasize a complete distortion or denial of the reality of death. Surely stories of this nature, no matter how meritorious in literary or artistic tone, should not be presented with the hope of helping a bereaved child deal with a death experience in his or her own life.

Similarly, *Across the Meadow*,[2] a picture book by Ben Shecter, tells the story of a cat who apparently goes across a meadow to die. Unfortunately, death in this story is equated with "going to sleep," a concept that might produce or reinforce numerous bedtime fears. Death is also described here as "going on vacation," another concept that might well exacerbate the difficulties involved in achieving an acceptance and understanding of the reality of death. In addition, equating "death" with "vacation" may well create heightened anxiety for young children whenever their own parents leave for vacation.

This raises an important issue to consider when viewing children's literature either as a means of encouraging communication between children and adults or as an aid in focusing attention on a particular topic such as death. In recommending juvenile books with such purposes in mind, it is necessary not only to become familiar with the children for whom the books are intended, but also to become familiar with the books themselves so that a wise and potentially helpful selection can be made. Recommending certain stories for certain children mainly because the selected stories appear to deal with topics currently important in a specific child's life, without carefully appraising the actual story material, involves a realistic danger. *A Boy, a Dog, a Frog and a Friend* and *Across the Meadow* are two publications that epitomize this danger.

---

[2] Shecter, Ben. *Across the Meadow*. Garden City, N.Y.: Doubleday, 1973.

Stories That Might Relate Well to Issues Surrounding Human Death

Stories Showing Warm Relationships Between Elderly Individuals and Young Children

The above examples from the field of children's literature all deal with nature, the death of pets, or the loss of other objects. There are, in addition, several books available today that touch sensitively on issues surrounding human death.

Books showing warm relationships between elderly individuals and young children are helpful here in order to focus attention initially on old age. *Grandmother and I* and *Grandfather and I,* both by Helen Buckley, portray such relationships, each suggesting by its warm and gentle tone that a grandparent and a young child may have much to share even though they are at very different stages in the cycle of life. *Grandpa and Me,* by Patricia Gauch, also portrays a valuable and mutually satisfying relationship between a young child and a grandparent.

More complex emotional and family reactions to old age are touched upon in *Matt's Grandfather,* by Max Lundgren, for here the elderly grandfather has been placed in an old-age home. When Matt comes to visit, he learns a little more about what being old is all about, but he also senses a spryness and an appealing charm in his eighty-five-year-old grandfather that his own parents apparently cannot or do not want to acknowledge.

Stories That Raise the Issue of Possible Death in the Near Future

Other books, such as *I Love Gram,* by Ruth Sonneborn, come somewhat closer to an actual death experience by introducing, in the story itself, concerns centering around the imminent or possible death of a beloved grandparent. Stories such as these can lead easily into discussions of old age and approaching death, often motivating children to tell about their own experiences with elderly relatives or friends. Helpful topics to raise in discussing this book include the reassuring fact that people usually live long lives—that the usual and most natural experience is for death to arrive some time in old age. It

is also valuable and often reassuring to inform a child that there will always be someone available to care for him or her no matter how many individuals important in his or her own life may unexpectedly die.

I Want Mama, by Marjorie W. Sharmat, explores a young child's feelings while her mother is in the hospital. It seems like her mother is away such a long time that the little girl begins to wonder sadly if she is ever going to come back at all. "Maybe," she thinks to herself, "if I promise to tell the whole truth for the rest of my life, Mama will come back."

Many of the feelings portrayed in this story illustrate the egocentric thinking of young children. For example, a child may mistakenly believe that a particular action or lack of action on his or her own part has actually caused, or is related to, a parent's illness. *I Want Mama* offers an excellent opportunity to explore and attempt to correct such serious misconceptions.

In *I Want Mama,* the mother does eventually return home. Feelings and fears surrounding her hospital stay are realistically portrayed. The story may be particularly meaningful to children currently facing their own parents' hospitalization or illness. Omitted from this book, however, is a portrayal of the mother's physical or emotional condition when she returns. The emphasis, instead, is on the child's own feelings and reactions throughout the story. It might be helpful, therefore, to suggest to a young child that often a mother returning from the hospital will be weak and tired for some time to come and will not, in all likelihood, be "the same as always" as rapidly as this story seems to suggest.

Stories Centering Around the Actual Death of a Person

Finally, there are several stories available today that center around the actual death of a person and the emotions surrounding that death. *Annie and the Old One,* by Miska Miles, is the story of Annie, a young Navajo girl who has a special and close relationship with her elderly grandmother. One day, Annie's grandmother announces that she expects to die by the time the rug comes from the loom. Then, because she doesn't want her grandmother to die, Annie desperately tries to prevent the completion of the rug. Again and again she devises a plan to interfere with the weaving. Finally, the grandmother discovers Annie's scheming. With a gentle but firm explanation she

helps her granddaughter understand that one cannot stop time or change what must be.

At one point in this story, Annie's mother expresses a reluctance to talk with her daughter about her grandmother's approaching death. "We will speak of other things," she tells Annie. Here is an excellent opportunity to help children understand that some adults are simply not able to talk about death in an open and honest manner (or are decidedly uncomfortable in doing so). Although children should be encouraged to express their own fears and feelings concerning death, they should also be helped to understand that the adults whom they meet will vary greatly in their propensity and willingness to talk freely about this topic.

Scat, by Arnold Dobrin, also treats death as a natural occurrence and emphasizes the fact that one can deal with death in whatever manner is personally most comforting. Scat, a young boy who loves jazz music, wants to acknowledge his grandmother's death in his own way. Therefore, after everyone has left the funeral services, Scat goes to a quiet spot near her grave, takes his harmonica out of his pocket, and begins to play.

My Grandpa Died Today, by Joan Fassler, portrays a warm and loving relationship between an elderly grandfather and a boy named David. As in the two stories discussed above, the grandparent here also senses that he will soon die. This story is based in large part on the work of Erik Erikson (1963). It portrays a grandfather who has apparently reached the last and final stage of his life span with feelings of acceptance and dignity, rather than bitterness and despair. Although the grandfather's death brings deep sadness and a sense of loss to those who loved him, the real emphasis in *My Grandpa Died Today* is, once again, on the ongoing nature of life itself. The story embodies, in part, the circular nature of life, as described by Erikson in his "Eight Ages of Man." For Erikson, there is a strong relationship between the sense of dignity or integrity achieved by certain individuals during the last stage of their development and the sense of basic trust to be achieved, if all goes well, during the first stage of human development. "Healthy children," Erikson states, "will not fear life, if their elders have integrity enough not to fear death" (1963, p. 269). *My Grandpa Died Today* is an attempt to illustrate this theme by showing an elderly man's peaceful acceptance of his own impending death and a young boy's strong commitment to life. It also attempts to show an open and honest expression of feelings, suggesting, among other things, that it is perfectly acceptable for men as well as women to cry and show emotion.

In response to stories centering around the death of a human being, children can be offered an opportunity to initially express their own feelings about the story material. They should also be given ample opportunity to talk openly, if they care to do so, about their own experiences with death. In addition, some leading questions might be presented as a means of encouraging further discussion. Questions such as the following, presented after reading *My Grandpa Died Today,* have been used successfully to initiate discussion about death among young children:

> How did David feel about his grandfather?
> Do you know anyone who is very old? How do you get along with that person?
> Was David responsible in any way for his grandfather's death?
> Why did David go out and play ball, even though he felt so sad?
> Will David's grandfather ever be able to play ball with him again?
> Have you ever lost anybody or anything that you loved very much? What did you do then and how did you feel?

When such questions are asked, the children involved must be helped to understand that there are no right or wrong answers. The adult participating in the discussion must be prepared to listen carefully and respectfully to any responses offered, and must also be careful not to demand a response from the child who chooses to remain silent. Children do respond to such questions, often surprising adults with the perspicacity of their comments. For example, when asked if it was good to cry if you were very, very sad, one six-year-old replied that crying was very important because there might be a jar of sadness filled with tears inside each person. "If the jar ever got too full," she suggested, "it would simply burst, and that would hurt too much." Crying, she thought, might let out just the right amount of sadness to relieve the pain. Other children have been eager to reveal, in great detail, burial procedures once initiated for long lost pets, with several children describing incidents their parents assumed had long since been forgotten.

It is not suggested that such discussion alone will solve a particular problem for a young child or banish anxiety about death. A child might, however, obtain some valuable emotional support and reassurance if he has been able to talk about death openly and honestly, if someone has listened seriously to his comments, and if he has been helped to understand that there are adults with whom he can explore the subject again if he should ever feel the need or the desire to do so.

In addition to initiating discussion, stories relating to death might motivate some children to draw pictures or model clay in a manner that best illustrates their own reactions to the story themes, or best expresses their own feelings and experiences with death. Others may choose to write (or dictate) an original story concerning death. Additionally, some children may want to learn about the various customs or traditions that different cultural or religious groups observe with respect to death. Interested children can be encouraged to share their knowledge in this area, too.

For children in therapy, stories about death might be made available, at the discretion of the therapist, to help a child explore feelings surrounding a particular death, or to help focus attention on the topic of death itself. Sometimes a therapist may want to recommend a particular story to a family coping with an actual death experience for use as an aid in initiating discussion within the family.

Two other picture books portraying the deaths of human beings have recently been published in the United States. *Sir Ribbeck of Ribbeck of Havelland,* written by Theodor Fontane, a popular children's-book author in Germany, has now been translated and published in an English edition. This story centers around the death of an elderly man. It might, however, be somewhat confusing to a young child because of its strong emphasis upon the man's attempt to provide fruit for the children of his community long after his death, despite the objections of his selfish and miserly son. After the old man is buried, a voice from his grave repeatedly urges the children of the village to come and taste a pear. This voice-from-the-grave concept may be confusing and difficult for young children to deal with, particularly if they have not yet established the irreversibility of death firmly in their own minds.

Nana Upstairs and Nana Downstairs, by Tomie de Paola, portrays the death of two elderly people—Tommy's great-grandmother and, later, his grandmother. Of special value here is the fact that Tommy verbalizes many questions concerning death and that his family encourages him to do so; also, they permit him to cry when he is sad, without belittling his tears. However, some points in this story, too, may be difficult for young children to handle: e.g., for some time before her death Tommy's great-grandmother is repeatedly tied into a chair to prevent her falling; also, after the deaths have occurred, Tommy is informed that a falling star might be a kiss from his grandparents, a belief that could, once again, confuse a young child who is first beginning to grasp the reality of death.

Used as the basis of a sensitive discussion, however, *Sir Ribbeck of Ribbeck of Havelland* and *Nana Upstairs and Nana Downstairs* can be helpful in focusing attention on fears and feelings surrounding death. In addition, if used wisely, both can furnish excellent opportunities for adults to correct some serious misconceptions a young child might have about death. For example, when discussing these books, the adult can emphasize the finality of death so that children can be helped to understand that a loved one who has died cannot return to the living (and cannot, in reality, send kisses or fruit, either), but that thoughts and memories concerning the deceased person *can* indeed remain with the living for a long, long time.

Stories About Children Who Have Experienced the Death or Loss of an Important Individual in Their Lives Sometime in the Past

Other books that might be helpful in encouraging a consideration of death among young children are those in which the storybook characters have experienced the death or loss of an individual important in their lives sometime in the past. Among these are *Sam, Bangs & Moonshine,* by Evaline Ness, *I Won't Go Without a Father,* by Muriel Stanek, and *A Father Like That,* by Charlotte Zolotow, each of which involves the loss of a parent or parent-figure sometime in the past. Zolotow's book is particularly useful in illustrating the fact that children are likely to create numerous fantasies centering around a parent who may have died or may have abandoned the family early in the child's life or even before the child was born. In this story, a young boy whose father "went away before he was born" is clearly but sensitively reminded that the father he is thinking about is indeed a fantasy-figure. "I like the kind of father you are talking about," the boy's mother tells him. Then she reminds her son that in case such a father never comes along, perhaps he can be a father like that, himself, when he grows up.

In *Sam, Bangs & Moonshine,* a little girl has difficulty in coming to terms with the reality of her mother's death, which apparently occurred some time ago. Repeated comments in pediatric and psychiatric literature acknowledge this phenomenon. Morris Wessel (1973), among others, has described how painful it can be for a child to withdraw his attachment to an adult, who, being dead, is no longer available as a person to whom the child can attach his love. Thus, he explains, children often discuss and appear to accept a death at one level of functioning, yet simultaneously deny it at another level. In this story, the girl's father finally helps her understand and acknowledge the difference between "real" and "moonshine,"—moonshine being the father's word for fantasy. At the same time, the father helps his daughter begin to face the reality of her mother's death.

I Won't Go Without a Father emphasizes the importance placed upon substitute relationships by a young boy who comes from a one-parent home and realistically touches upon some of the inner feelings of anger, loneliness, and jealousy that may exist in such a situation.

Books dealing with adoption or portraying children in foster family settings also, by their very nature, suggest the loss of a biological parent some time in the past. A discussion of such books will be found in Chapter IV.

Information-Type Books About Death

Several juvenile books available today offer information about death. For example, *Talking About Death,* by Earl Grollman, proposes a dialogue for parents and children on the topic of death. There is no story or plot presented here. Grollman's book is simply an open and honest attempt to explain death to young children. For the most part, the points raised are psychologically sound. In fact, Grollman zeroes in on some of the most crucial concerns that are likely to enter a child's mind if a death should occur in his or her family:

Are you worried that you did something wrong and that is why grandfather died?
Was his death a punishment to you?
Were you mean to him and did your meanness cause his death?
Are you angry that grandfather died?

Grollman also offers children numerous realistic comments about death. "DEAD is DEAD," he tells them. "It is not a game. It is very real." Again and again, Grollman urges his readers to say the words DEAD and DIE aloud. "That's what happened to grandfather," he tells them. "Grandfather died. He is dead."

I would, however, have some serious misgivings about recommending this book to be read aloud to small children, as the book jacket suggests. Being strictly a "lesson" in death, the book might present more truth in one publication than young children can handle comfortably. The total effect, therefore, could be a frightening one. In addition, the author does not offer the kind of reassurances that could be most helpful in reducing the possibility of an anxiety-laden response to his book. For example, he does not note that most people do, in fact, live a long time; that the child reader and his parents, too, will probably live for a long time; and that there will *always* be someone available to care for the child if a close family member should die. Perhaps most lacking, however, is a quality called "distancing." Simon Lesser (1957) describes this distancing factor as a means of separating a story from the reader by a reassuring space, for the story, after all, is something that is happening to storybook characters. It is exactly this distancing quality found in fiction, Lesser suggests, that enables a reader to deal with the more painful events of a story, both as a spectator and as an emotional participant, without creating undue anxiety. Grollman's book, on the contrary, presents a series of statements about death, one after another, without offering any storybook characters as intermediaries. This is another reason why *Talking About Death*, though including many psychologically sound statements, may heighten anxiety, particularly in young children. Older children, more experienced in meeting or perhaps talking about death, might be better able to deal with the subject as presented here—in Grollman's bold, stark, realistic style.

A newer edition of Grollman's book (1976) includes an expanded Parent's Guide and additional important bibliographic information. The difficulties discussed here, however, have not been satisfactorily resolved in the children's portion.

Talking About Death does offer excellent material for parents to read and absorb themselves. In fact, Grollman's book might be most valuable when used as a resource guide for adults to help them understand more about children's reactions and fears concerning death. At the same time, it can help adults achieve a deeper understanding of their own attitudes and concerns regarding death. Most importantly, it may help parents (and other adults) overcome a reluctance to talk about death openly and honestly with children.

Life and Death, by Herbert S. Zim and Sonia Bleeker, another information-type book, is directed toward older children. This book is highly scientifically oriented, dealing mainly with those issues surrounding death that can be answered by simple factual statements. It does not deal with the many emotional issues concerning death—

issues that Grollman's book acknowledges clearly and honestly. *Life and Death* does, however, describe various beliefs and customs concerning death in a straightforward and simple manner. It could, therefore, be a useful source book for adults. For example, one mother reported that her own exposure to the explanation of cremation in the Zim and Bleeker book was particularly helpful when she later attempted to answer difficult questions posed by her child in response to the sudden death and cremation of the child's grandparent.

About Dying, by Sara Bonnett Stein, is another information-type book about death, presented in a novel format which includes a text for children and a separate text for adults on each page. The adult text is, in fact, an excellent resource guide concerning children's reactions to death. The children's text, directed to preschool and primary-grade children, presents a realistic child's-eye view of death, first the death of a bird, then the death of a grandfather. The book includes large, realistic photographs, one, for example, showing a child next to a coffin and another showing a cemetery scene. Much of the material covered in the Grollman book is found here too, but children's feelings about death are perhaps explored even more deeply in the Stein book. The sharing of this book by children and adults could present a valuable opportunity to focus attention on many of the feelings, fears, fantasies, and misunderstandings that are likely to exist in a young child's mind concerning death.

Reviews of this book in library journals have suggested that the combined approach here—two different texts on each page, one intended for children and one for adults—is far too complicated a form for a juvenile book. The adult text, however, offers valuable information concerning children and death, often presenting specific suggestions for helping children cope with death that parents, for example, may not easily obtain elsewhere. At the same time, the vivid photographs and simple, though slight, story line, seem intriguing enough to hold a child's interest. The format, though unusual, does not seem to disturb children as much as it disturbs reviewers.

About Dying should not, however, be urged upon a child as a lesson in death. It should, instead, be shared with an adult, preferably one who is wise enough and flexible enough to adapt the material, when necessary, in accordance with a child's own developmental needs and resources. The child should be given ample opportunity to raise questions and express his or her own feelings concerning death. Used in this manner, as a communicative-aid, *About Dying* may be an excellent choice to help children develop and maintain the inner strength needed to cope with painful events, not as they imagine them to be, but as they truly are.

When a Child Dies

Books About the Death (or Threatened Death) of a Child

The death of a child is always a devastating experience. The intricacies of relationships between children who are dying, hospital staff, and parents have been sensitively described by a number of researchers (Schowalter, 1971; Solnit, 1959, 1973; Vernick, 1973). Elisabeth Kübler-Ross (1975), in her lectures and writings, has focused attention on different stages of dying, brilliantly illustrating the symbolic language dying patients (including children) have offered in drawings and speech in an attempt to communicate feelings at the various stages.

Juvenile books portraying the death of a child are usually presented at the junior-high-school or high-school reading and interest level. There is a great paucity of books at the preschool and primary-grade level dealing with this subject. Physicians, nurses, social workers, friends, and family members facing a child's death have asked me, from time to time, to recommend books that might portray some of the anxieties and feelings surrounding the death of a young person. Occasionally, a book dealing with the death of a child has proven modestly helpful at such times.

One of the most useful books for this purpose is *A Taste of Blackberries,* by Doris B. Smith. In this story, the young narrator initially expresses denial, grief, and guilt in response to the unexpected death of his close friend. His parents offer physical comfort, emotional support, and simple, honest explanations. They communicate about death in a straightforward and realistic manner, thus helping their son accept the occurrence of death and deal effectively with the feelings it evokes.

Hang Tough, Paul Mather, by Alfred Slote, also presents a realistic view of a difficult situation. This is the sensitive story of Paul, a twelve-year-old boy struggling to cope with, and combat, leukemia. Paul's feelings and perceptions concerning his own incurable illness are vividly portrayed. Fear of death, anger about being sick, dislike of the treatment and its side effects are some of the emotions Paul shares with an understanding doctor. The family, too, is realistically portrayed. Although this story does not include an actual death, it does deal with feelings aroused by the threat of death. The book might help adults gain a deeper understanding of a child's point of view concerning a potentially fatal illness.

Books of this nature should be recommended only by someone who knows a family and a situation well, particularly if a child's death is currently anticipated. Such books can also be helpful to friends and family long after a specific death has occurred. Martha Wolfenstein (Wolfenstein and Kliman, 1965) reports the incident of a young boy who was unable to cry when his own mother died, but some time later cried profusely when he read about the death of his favorite fictional characters, the Three Musketeers. Wolfenstein calls this phenomenon "mourning at a distance." The two books described here may, in a similar manner, encourage the release of some pent-up feelings concerning a past experience with death.

Death Among Anthropomorphized Animals

Charlotte's Web, by E. B. White, contains one of the most poignant death experiences in juvenile literature. Second- and third-graders are often quite familiar with Charlotte, a spider, and Wilbur, a pig, as this book is frequently read aloud (by librarians and teachers alike) during the early primary grades. When Charlotte uses her weaving and writing skills to spin the words SOME PIG! and TERRIFIC across Wilbur's pen in the hope of saving Wilbur from the slaughtering house, children are delighted with her accomplishment. Later, when Charlotte herself dies, children recognize that Wilbur has indeed lost a good friend:

> *Wilbur never forgot Charlotte. Although he loved her children and grandchildren dearly, none of the new spiders ever quite took her place in his heart. She was in a class by herself. It is not often that someone comes along who is a true friend and a good writer. Charlotte was both. (p. 184)*

A child who has experienced the death of a friend may find some comfort in discovering, through books like *Charlotte's Web*, that feelings of loss and sadness are universal, but that life does indeed go on.

Conclusion

In all likelihood, the books and stories discussed in this chapter will be most helpful if they are used as catalysts for the expression of feelings between children and adults—if they can be used to help focus attention on some important issues surrounding death, possibly shedding light on a young child's feelings, fantasies, and misconceptions about death. Used in this manner, books concerning death, and the discussions they initiate, might help children grasp some important concepts:

Death is a topic that can be talked about;
One's emotions about death, or about someone who has died, can and should be expressed;
It is perfectly all right to cry when something sad occurs;
The death of a loved one is not due to any wrongdoing or evil thought on the part of the child;
The usual, most natural experience is for death to arrive some time in old age; and
There will always be someone available to care for a child if a death should occur within his or her family.

Facing death through literature can sometimes initiate a story–child–adult interaction process that is highly rewarding. Adults observing or participating in this process may be surprised to discover that books can encourage mastery of some of life's most difficult experiences, for stories *can* and *do* help children grow.

References

BOWLBY, J., and PARKES, M. Separation and loss within the family. *International Yearbook for Child Psychiatry and Allied Disciplines,* 1970, *1,* 197–216.

ERIKSON, E. H. *Childhood and society* (2nd ed.). New York: W. W. Norton, 1963.

FURMAN, R. A. The child's reaction to death in the family. In B. Schoenberg, A. C. Carr, D. Peretz, and A. H. Kutscher (Eds.), *Loss and grief: Psychological management in medical practice.* New York: Columbia University Press, 1970.

GROLLMAN, E. A. *Explaining death to children*. Boston: Beacon Press, 1967.

KLIMAN, G. *Psychological emergencies of childhood*. New York: Grune & Stratton, 1968.

KÜBLER-ROSS, E. *Death: The final stage of growth*. Englewood Cliffs, N.J.: Prentice-Hall, 1975.

LANES, S. G. *Down the rabbit hole: Adventures and misadventures in the realm of children's literature*. New York: Atheneum, 1971.

LESSER, S. O. *Fiction and the unconscious*. New York: Random House, 1957.

NAGERA, H. Children's reactions to the death of important objects: A developmental approach. *The Psychoanalytic Study of the Child*, 1970, *25*, 360–99.

SOLNIT, A. J., and GREEN, M. Psychological considerations in the management of deaths on pediatric hospital services: The doctor and the child's family. *Pediatrics*, 1959, *24* (1), 106–22.

SOLNIT, A. J. Who mourns when a child dies? In E. J. Anthony and C. Koupernik (Eds.), *The child in his family: The impact of disease and death* (vol. 2). New York: John Wiley & Sons, 1973.

SCHOWALTER, J. E. Death and the pediatric nurse. *Journal of Thanatology*, 1971, *1*(2), 81–90.

VERNICK, J. Meaningful communication with the fatally ill child. In E. J. Anthony and C. Koupernik (Eds.) *The child in his family: The impact of disease and death* (vol. 2). New York: John Wiley & Sons, 1973.

WESSEL, M. A. Death of an adult—and its impact upon the child. *Clinical Pediatrics*, 1973, *12*(1), 28–33.

WOLFENSTEIN, M. The impact of a children's story on mothers and children. *Monographs of the Society for Research in Child Development*, 1947, *11*(1).

WOLFENSTEIN, M., and KLIMAN, G. *Children and the death of a president*. New York: Doubleday, 1965.

Juvenile Bibliography: Books That Might Help Young Children Talk About or Share Some Feelings Concerning Death

Stories About Nature and Change

KRAUSS, RUTH. *The Growing Story*. Illus. by Phyllis Rowand. New York: Harper & Row, 1947.

KUSKIN, KARLA. *The Bear Who Saw the Spring.* New York: Harper & Row, 1961.

McCLOSKEY, ROBERT. *Time of Wonder.* New York: Viking Press, 1957.

TRESSELT, ALVIN. *White Snow, Bright Snow.* Illus. by Roger Duvoisin. New York: Lothrop, Lee & Shepard, 1947.

Stories About the Death of Pets or Loss of Other Objects

BROWN, MARGARET WISE. *The Dead Bird.* Illus. By Remy Charlip. Reading, Mass.: Addison-Wesley, Young Scott Books, 1938, 1965.

LAMORISSE, ALBERT. *The Red Balloon.* Transl. from the French by Ferris Mack. Garden City, N.Y.: Doubleday, 1956.

VIORST, JUDITH. *The Tenth Good Thing About Barney.* Illus. by Erik Blegvad. New York: Atheneum, 1971.

WARBURG, SANDOL. *Growing Time.* Illus. by Leonard Weisgard. Boston: Houghton Mifflin, 1969.

Stories That Might Relate Well to Issues Surrounding Human Death

Stories Showing Warm Relationships Between Elderly Individuals and Young Children

BUCKLEY, HELEN. *Grandfather and I.* Illus. by Paul Galdone. New York: Lothrop, Lee & Shepard, 1959.

BUCKLEY, HELEN. *Grandmother and I.* Illus. by Paul Galdone. New York: Lothrop, Lee & Shepard, 1961.

GAUCH, PATRICIA. *Grandpa and Me.* Illus. by Symeon Shimin. New York: Coward, McCann & Geoghegan, 1972.

LUNDGREN, MAX. *Matt's Grandfather.* Illus. by Fibben Hald. Transl. from the Swedish by Ann Pyk. New York: G. P. Putnam's Sons, 1972.

Stories That Raise the Issue of Possible Death in the Near Future

SHARMAT, MARJORIE W. *I Want Mama.* Illus. by Emily McCully. New York: Harper & Row, 1974.

SONNEBORN, RUTH. *I Love Gram.* Illus. by Leo Carty. New York: Viking Press, 1971.

Stories Centering Around the Actual Death of a Person

DE PAOLA, TOMIE. *Nana Upstairs and Nana Downstairs.* New York: G. P. Putnam's Sons, 1973.

DOBRIN, ARNOLD. *Scat.* New York: Four Winds Press, 1971.

FASSLER, JOAN. *My Grandpa Died Today.* Illus. by Stuart Kranz. New York: Behavioral Publications, 1971.

FONTANE, THEODOR. *Sir Ribbeck of Ribbeck of Havelland.* Illus. by Nonny Hogrogian. Transl. from the German by Elizabeth Shub. New York: Macmillan, 1969.

MILES, MISKA. *Annie and the Old One.* Illus. by Peter Parnall. Boston: Little, Brown, 1971.

Stories About Children Who Have Experienced the Death or Loss of an Important Individual in Their Lives Sometime in the Past

NESS, EVALINE. *Sam, Bangs and Moonshine.* New York: Holt, Rinehart & Winston, 1966.

STANEK, MURIEL. *I Won't Go Without a Father.* Illus. by Eleanor Mill. Chicago: Albert Whitman, 1972.

ZOLOTOW, CHARLOTTE. *A Father Like That.* Illus. by Ben Shecter. New York: Harper & Row, 1971.

Information-Type Books About Death

GROLLMAN, EARL A. *Talking About Death: A Dialogue Between Parent and Child.* Illus. by Gisela Héau. Boston: Beacon Press, 1970, 1976.

STEIN, SARA BONNETT. *About Dying.* Photographs by Dick Frank. New York: Walker, 1974.

ZIM, HERBERT S., and BLEEKER, SONIA. *Life and Death.* Illus. by Rene Martin. New York: William Morrow, 1970.

When a Child Dies

Books About the Death (or Threatened Death) of a Child

SLOTE, ALFRED. *Hang Tough, Paul Mather.* Philadelphia: J. B. Lippincott, 1973.

SMITH, DORIS B. *A Taste of Blackberries.* Illus. by Charles Robinson. New York: Thomas Y. Crowell, 1973.

Stories About Death Among Anthropomorphized Animals

WHITE, E. B. *Charlotte's Web.* Illus. by Garth Williams. New York: Harper & Row, 1952.

II

Separation Experiences

NUMEROUS REPORTS CONCERNING children's fears list separation fear (fear of being separated from one's parents for various reasons) as one of the strongest fears of early childhood (Berger, 1971; Goodenough, 1963). One researcher, Dr. John Bowlby, a distinguished British psychiatrist and psychoanalyst, has made his life-work the study of the effects of separation from one or both parents upon young children, including separations involving brief intervals. In a recent publication, Bowlby (1973) argues that a child's emotional life has one simple, solemn theme—the need for closeness to the mother. All anxiety, he suggests, is a "realistic" fear of separation from the mother. Much of the child's unfolding personality and much pathology, too, Bowlby believes, can be explained in terms of the need to defend against the threat of loss or separation.

Most researchers studying the effects of separation experiences on young children would agree that favorable experiences that help children achieve mastery of separation anxiety, as well as unfavorable experiences that tend to create new anxieties or exacerbate existing separation fears, can all have a strong influence upon further development.

Separation fears and anxieties are universal experiences for young children. Nursery-school teachers are quite familiar with the emotional reactions three- and four-year-old children experience as they attempt to cope with separation from their parents, each according to his or her own style or stage of development (Furman, 1966; Gross, 1970; Kessler et al., 1969). Today it is often suggested that the initial separation of parent and child for school purposes should be achieved in a gradual manner, with both mother and child spending some time together in the school setting, and with children being given ample opportunity to become accustomed to a new school situation by means of gradually increased periods of separation (Speers et al., 1971).

For very young children, separation from a parent, even a brief and well-planned separation, is seldom a simple matter. Anna Freud (1965) has noted that children must first develop some form of object constancy before they can realize that a mother's departure does not mean total loss. With further development, the need for adjustment to separation from one's parents does not suddenly stop; it continues as an ongoing process, a normal and often-repeated experience in a children's life (Pine, 1971). As part of this ongoing process, it has been suggested that successful adjustment to one type of separation experience (such as staying for brief periods of time with a well-known and trusted baby-sitter) at one stage of development may help a child develop the inner resources needed to cope with future separation experiences (such as attending nursery or primary school).

It is also possible that reading and discussing carefully selected stories with young children might offer some help in this area of early child development. Previous reports have indicated that the presentation of stories, followed by opportunities for story discussion, can affect the behavior and attitudes of young children (Kimmel, 1970; Meathenia, 1971; Webster, 1961). Similar effects regarding separation experiences may also be possible. For example, some children might gain comfort from seeing that other children, even storybook children (or animals), often feel just as they do about new situations involving separations from their parents, and that their own actions and fears regarding such separations are not shameful and can be mastered gradually. Other children may be reassured to discover that most storybook children do eventually overcome their hesitancies and do move on to more independent behavior. Reassuring, also, might be the fact that in the selected stories, parents and children are always reunited after brief periods of planned and unplanned separations. In addition, some children may feel particularly proud to discover that they have already accomplished the very separation-type task that a storybook character is still struggling to master. Most importantly, such stories can offer children and adults excellent opportunities to share some honest feelings and air some inner concerns regarding a variety of early separation experiences in a potentially helpful and growth-producing manner.

The juvenile publications discussed in this chapter have been selected because of the manner in which they seem to relate to several common separation-type experiences of early childhood. The stories described, and the discussions they generate, can, I believe, be particularly useful for children and parents who are presently making an initial adjustment to an early school experience or for children who will be facing a first school experience in the near future. They can also be helpful in introducing children to the idea of separation in general. More specifically, they offer an excellent vehicle for consideration of a child's own fears and fantasies concerning bedtime separations, staying with a baby-sitter, accidental or unexpected separations, necessary separations from well-liked friends or trusted adults, sleeping away from home, and similar separation-type experiences. Materials concerning separation for purposes involving hospitalization, death or divorce are not included in the present chapter, as such topics appear to merit individual attention in their own right.

It is hoped that the wise and sensitive use of the selected materials described here will help some children achieve a greater degree of mastery regarding separation anxieties, an achievement that will be called upon, again and again, throughout their lives.

Reassuring Stories To Help Counteract Fears of Abandonment

A helpful introduction to early separation can sometimes be achieved by means of sharing a reassuring, well-liked story with a young child, particularly a story in which parent and child are consistently and warmly reunited after brief, even momentary, separations. The early use of such stories can help reinforce the idea of object constancy, e.g., that mother still exists and has not permanently abandoned her child, even though she is momentarily out of sight. Several long-time favorites in the children's book field offer excellent opportunities for adults and children to focus their attention together, in a positive, nonthreatening manner, on such brief separation experiences. In *The Bundle Book*, by Ruth Krauss, an empathetic mother exhibits some playful puzzlement as she engages in a guessing game with her small daughter. Finally, she discovers that the mysterious bundle on her bed is simply a blanket, hiding exactly what she wants and needs most of all—her own little girl. Besides being fun to read, this story can serve to emphasize the fact that even though an inanimate object, such as a blanket, might temporarily separate parent and child from each other's view, abandonment has not taken place. Instead, real-life children, like the storybook child, can eventually learn to expect and depend upon their parents' reappearance whenever games of this type take place. A somewhat similar theme is explored in *The Runaway Bunny,* by Margaret Wise Brown. Here a small bunny and his mother engage in an imaginary game of verbal hide-and-seek as they consider together the many different hiding places a runaway bunny might select. First published in 1942, this book has been well-received by two generations of young readers (or story-listeners). Perhaps children find special comfort in discovering that the bunny and his mother are always reunited after each make-believe separation.

Children sometimes fear that their own misbehavior may initiate parental abandonment. In Miriam Schlein's book, *The Way Mothers Are,* a mother cat unequivocally loves her kitten, not because he is good or clever, or because he draws nice pictures, but simply because he is her very own kitten (child). Especially reassuring here is the fact that this mother's love is not offered or withdrawn because of good or naughty behavior on the kitten's part; it is, instead, a dependable, consistent emotion.

Books of this nature are apt to encourage repeated readings and dramatic play, as young children often want to hear the stories over and over again, often imitating the characters portrayed here. Such activities, centering around a familiar storybook situation, can help children learn that brief separations will occur again and again, and that experiences involving separation can indeed be met and mastered gradually.

Bedtime Stories

Gentle Stories To Help Relax a Child at Bedtime

Nighttime separation from parents begins at a very early age in the United States. The nursery-school-aged child will, in all likelihood, have developed various coping mechanisms for facing the temporary separation from parents that the arrival of night (or the expectations of the adults in his or her environment) seems to necessitate. A simple, reassuring, bedtime story, shared at night with an understanding parent, can often play an important role in helping a young child

master separation from parents at bedtime. Favorites with young children seem to be those bedtime books that are very much the same, page after page, such as *Goodnight Moon,* by Margaret Wise Brown. This book presents a soothing transition from day to night as a small rabbit looks around his room and says goodnight to all the familiar things he sees. As the night grows darker, the rabbit's room and even the pages of the story gradually grow darker, too. Softly, the rabbit whispers goodnight to clocks and socks, to kittens and mittens, and to a picture of three little bears sitting in three little chairs. He says goodnight to his room and to the moon, to the stars and to the air, and finally, to noises everywhere.

Although *Goodnight Moon* does not touch on any underlying anxieties, it does seem to have a pleasing, soporific effect on small children. *Goodnight Moon* has, in fact, been selected again and again as a favorite bedtime book by three- to five-year-old children (and their families) ever since its first printing in 1947.

A somewhat similar, sleep-inducing theme is found in *Sleepy Book,* by Charlotte Zolotow, a picture book whose story is first introduced by a yawning child. *Sleepy Book* then proceeds, in a low-keyed, drowsy kind of way, to show how birds and beasts and little girls and boys all go to sleep, each in his or her own way. For slightly older children, *While Susie Sleeps,* by Nina Schneider, tells about some interesting things that go on right through the night while Susie sleeps, such as the continuous movement of traffic, the baking of bread in bakeries, the printing of the morning newspaper and a cat taking a quiet walk down the block. Then, as morning arrives, Susie and the world around her slowly begin to awake.

Stories Portraying Some Inner Concerns and Anxieties Surrounding Bedtime

Moving away from simple reassurance, there are a number of bedtime books that concentrate on some of the more complex issues surrounding bedtime. Nagera (1966) offers excellent background material for parents or professionals who want to learn more about sleep and its disturbances in early childhood. In *Lisa Cannot Sleep,* by Kaj Beckman, a young girl begins her bedtime routine by taking her favorite doll to bed. Subsequently, Lisa calls for and demands the addition, one by one, of so many toy animals that there is no longer room in bed for Lisa. Finally, with her mother's help, Lisa removes one animal after another, settling once again for her favorite and most comforting doll. It is often difficult for children to give up exciting daytime activities and relinquish contact with their parents, too, for the customary loneliness and seclusion of bed. Like Lisa, many children have a favorite toy or perhaps a "special" blanket that helps them make this transition.

Benjy's Blanket, by Myra B. Brown, explores the favorite-object theme even more directly. For some time Benjy's old, worn blanket has been his constant daytime and nighttime companion. Finally, when he himself feels that he no longer needs this special blanket, Benjy begins to forget it, leaving the blanket behind wherever he goes. Eventually Benjy gives his blanket to a newborn kitten who, he decides, really needs a special blanket of his own.

Both *Lisa Cannot Sleep* and *Benjy's Blanket* portray feelings easily recognized by young children. Both books can be used to encourage discussion about the commonly expressed need for a reassuring toy or blanket at bedtime. *Benjy's Blanket* might also be useful as a springboard for discussion at a parents' meeting to help focus attention on the meaning of various "transitional objects" in the lives of young children.

Other bedtime books concentrate on nighttime fantasies and fears. In *Goodnight Richard Rabbit,* by Robert Kraus, a small rabbit calls his mother again and again at bedtime, offering numerous excuses for his inability to fall asleep. Among his verbal concerns, Richard Rabbit suspects that there is a giant walking around downstairs, someone at the window, and an elephant in his bed. The gentle tone of the book and the nonthreatening nature of the pictures somewhat reduce the fears expressed by these fantasies. Although the mother rabbit is reasonably warm and reassuring, she does not equivocate about bedtime. Finally, Richard Rabbit goes to sleep. Here is a story that might be useful in helping a young child express fears or fantasies about bedtime. Children may discover that nighttime worries become much less troublesome if they are shared with an understanding adult, particularly an adult who can listen carefully in a calm, accepting manner, showing that he or she is not at all frightened by the child's fears.

More frightening nighttime fantasies also appear in children's books. Since young children still have difficulty understanding the difference between what is real and what is make-believe, such stories are not likely to encourage relaxation at bedtime in the preschool-age child and, in fact, might exacerbate any nighttime fears or anxieties the child may already have. A five- or six-year-old, however, may be able to understand that storybook "monsters" are only make-believe and may, in fact, gain some inner strength from discovering that he or she can read about and even master such scary-looking creatures.

Bedtime for Frances, by Russell Hoban, might be a good choice for a first-grader (and an adult) who would like to try a slightly scary bedtime story together. In this story, Frances, a small animal, imagines that there are many frightening things in her room at nighttime, several of which look like monsters or giants. Finally, Frances accepts her parents' gentle, but matter-of-fact, reassurance, and goes to sleep. Somewhat older children may prefer *There's a Nightmare in My Closet,* by Mercer Mayer, or *Goodnight Orange Monster,* by Betty Jean Lifton. These books may help children in the six- to eight-year age range talk about their fears and feelings concerning imaginary nighttime monsters. In both books, the endings are reassuring. In one, the child masters and eventually befriends the scary-looking creature; in the other, the young child grows up and grows out of his fear of monsters. In both cases, the distancing quality of the storybook situation can be useful in encouraging discussion between parents and children about bedtime fears in general, and their own child's fears in particular.

Frequently a child will encounter bedtime difficulties when other occurrences in his or her life are causing unusual anxiety or tension, such as the birth of a baby in the family, the illness or death of someone close to the child, or a move to a new home. A carefully selected book relating to one of these occurrences might be useful at such times as a springboard for discussion.[1] Sharing such a story with an understanding adult may help a child express fears or feelings that could be interfering with sleep, or may help a family keep the channels of communication open at a time when understanding is most needed.

Stories About Dreams and Dreaming

There are, in addition, several picture books of the bedtime genre that deal with dreams. Such books, too, can sometimes be useful as a background for helpful discussion between parents and children. First, children can be helped to understand that everyone has dream experiences. It can be highly reassuring for a young child to learn that dreams of varying kinds are an expected part of sleep. Books about dreams can also be used to help a child examine, with an understanding adult, the confusing difference between what is real and what is

---

[1] See Chapter IV for a discussion of books relating to such crisis-type occurrences, and Chapters I and III for books relating to death and hospitalization.

not real. In addition, stories about dreams sometimes help children verbalize personal feelings or concerns about their own dream experiences. Talking about dream sensations with an empathetic adult may, in turn, help reduce the fears engendered by such experiences. It is important, however, that a child sharing dreams or nighttime fantasies with an adult be quietly and warmly reassured, and not ridiculed in any way for the dream material, feelings, or fantasies he or she may express.

Did You Ever Dream?, by Doris Lund, is one of the simpler, more gentle dream books. This book could be used to initiate helpful discussion about dreams with five- to eight-year-old children. Other dream books that could be used to help focus attention upon the phenomena of dreaming per se or encourage discussion of actual dream experiences include: *A Child's Book of Dreams*, by Beatrice Schenk de Regniers; *I Have a Horse of My Own*, by Charlotte Zolotow; *The Children's Dream Book*, by Friedrich C. Heller; and *Amanda Dreaming*, by Barbara Wersba. In appreciation of the complexity of the meaning and interpretation of dreams, however, it might be important to comment, when sharing such books with young children, that often a specific nighttime dream cannot be related to an earlier daytime experience as simply and clearly as some of these books seem to suggest.

Although children should be offered opportunities to talk about their dreams, they should not be coerced into sharing dream material if they do not wish to do so. Acknowledgment of a child's right to privacy concerning dreams can be found in the de Regniers book. In this story, a mother inquires about her son's dream. "Yes, it was a good dream," the boy replies. "And maybe you tell them about your dream and maybe you don't," the author adds. Dreams, after all, belong to the dreamer and can, and should, be shared only when the dreamer is amenable to doing so.

Separation-Type Stories That Might Relate Well to Early School Experiences

Sometimes a book can help prepare a child for the separation to be encountered at the beginning of a new school experience. Charlotte Steiner's *I'd Rather Stay with You* is an excellent example. The baby kangaroo in this story doesn't want to leave his mother's pouch. "I'd rather stay with you," is his constant response to any suggestion that he undertake more independent activity. Finally, with the aid of his encouraging mother and the lure of a bright red balloon, the young kangaroo does manage to step out of the protective pouch. Later, he makes a tentative try at kindergarten and, apparently, enjoys school after all.

Of special significance here is the portrayal of a patient and understanding mother who doesn't abruptly push her child out of the pouch before he is ready to handle an independent experience. At the same time, when her offspring finally does appear ready for greater independence, his mother doesn't attempt to hold him back because of any of her own personal insecurities. Children can easily identify with the young kangaroo in this story, while mothers of preschool children would do well to take note of some of Mrs. Kangaroo's repetitive, encouraging, and confident behavior.

Jane Thayer's *A Drink for Little Red Diker* can also be used to help accustom young children to the idea of separation. Diker, a little red antelope, wishes that he were big enough and brave enough to go places by himself. After several timid and unsuccessful trials, he finally walks all the way through the forest to the lake, where he manages to get a drink of cool, refreshing water. However, in this story, the little antelope must first convince his own mother that he is indeed big enough to do things on his own. Although he is apparently quite ready to engage in certain independent activities, his mother seems to be somewhat reluctant to let him try.

Some children entering nursery school, kindergarten, or first grade may have a similar problem—a parent who is not quite ready to let a child grow up. It is frequently noted in the professional literature that separation problems are often parent problems. Perhaps children of such parents will view Little Red Diker's story as a kind of whispered encouragement toward the establishment of their own increasing readiness for more and more independent activities.

A similar vote for independence is found in Taro Yashima's well-loved story, *Umbrella*. Enthusiasm for a gift received on her third birthday, a brand new umbrella and a pair of bright red rain boots, encourages Momo to take an independent step. At the first sign of rain, she walks all the way to nursery school, and all the way back home a step ahead of her parents, without holding onto a grown-up's hand for security.

Several stories that take place inside actual school settings also illustrate some realistic separation feelings. In *Will I Have a Friend?*, by Miriam Cohen, a little boy named Jim, a newcomer to the neighborhood, is reluctant to be separated from his father on his first day at school. This story shows some of Jim's anxieties and his initial feeling of loneliness at the new school. Many child readers will understand exactly how Jim feels, and they will, in all likelihood, be happy to discover that he does manage to find a potential friend among his new classmates. By the end of the first day, Jim seems to feel more comfortable and more relaxed about school. Later that same day, the quiet confidence in Jim expressed by his father, serves to reinforce Jim's positive feelings about the new school.

Although written in a sensitive manner, and enjoyed by teachers and children alike, this story might have been considerably more helpful with regard to early separation experiences if it had portrayed, or at least suggested, the gradual nature of Jim's adjustment to the new school. Child readers (or story-listeners) might benefit from discussing this point and from considering the fact that it often takes a longer period of time than Jim's story seems to suggest for young children to adjust to new school situations.

The Two Friends, by Grete Mannheim, also portrays a young child's first day at school, and offers a brief glimpse of the next day as well. Some realistic feelings are expressed here in both story and photographs. Jenny admits that she is a bit afraid of so many strange children. She feels scared and lonely at first. Then, as in the previous story, finding a potential friend helps Jenny feel somewhat better about the whole situation.

Once again, the gradual nature of adjustment to school plays no part in this otherwise sensitive story. Certain problems and anxieties that may arise when a young child first enters school are indeed acknowledged in *The Two Friends.* Unfortunately, such concerns appear to be resolved much too rapidly here. In using this book with young children, it may be valuable, therefore, to follow the story with a frank discussion about the more extended period of time that is often needed to help a young child feel comfortable in a new school setting.

In *Cathy's First School,* by Betty Katzoff, sensitive photographs help tell the story of Cathy and her classmates. Most of the experiences described are happy ones, but one boy does momentarily burst into tears. Cathy, too, clearly expresses some temporarily hurt feelings. Since the story takes place on Cathy's sixth birthday, it ends with a class birthday party, complete with a number of handmade presents.

The portrayal of Cathy's first school in this story is both a happy and a realistic one. Cathy's story might help young children discuss

some of their own school experiences. At the same time, children who have not yet attended school might be motivated by Cathy's story to role-play what they think their own future school experiences will be like.

Shawn Goes to School, a short, simple, beautifully illustrated story, also describes a first school experience. This story, by Petronella Breinberg, focuses attention on a small black boy's first day at nursery school, realistically acknowledging his initial fear and shyness. After a while, Shawn becomes interested in the school's activities and begins to relate to the teacher who reminds him of his own aunt. Gradually, he relaxes and "smiles a teeny-weeny smile." Then Shawn's mother and his big brother, who together have brought him to the nursery school, decide that this is the right time to leave, and that is exactly what they do. Although I would prefer to see the portrayal of a much more gradual separation between parent and child, this book has been helpful in encouraging discussion among young children about starting nursery school, about what a child might expect to find there, and about the kinds of feelings an initial school experience might generate. I would, however, strongly recommend that an adult sharing this story with a young child suggest that often mommies and daddies arrange to stay at nursery school along with their children for just as long as the children (and their teachers) seem to need or want them to stay.

I Am Here: Yo Estoy Aqui, by Rose Blue, tells the story of Luz, a little Puerto Rican girl who attends kindergarten for the first time. Adjusting to a new country, a new school, and a new language is indeed difficult. Of special interest here is the suggestion of a warm and supportive relationship that is soon established between Luz and an assistant teacher who speaks Spanish. It is this relationship that helps Luz feel more comfortable at school and more confident about her own role in the classroom.

This story raises two important points regarding early school experiences. One is the frequent scarcity of bilingual adults in those classrooms where their presence could be of much potential value. In this respect, the story of Luz could serve as a valuable catalyst for the encouragement of greater participation in school activities by parents and other volunteers with bilingual skills. Perhaps, then, more children who do not understand much English will find, just as Luz did, a special kind of support and reassurance waiting for them in their new American classrooms.

Secondly, this story can help remind children, and parents as well, that there is likely to be a warm, pleasant, likeable adult in the classroom. Few stories portraying an initial school experience emphasize adult–child relationships. Emphasis is usually placed, instead, on materials and on relationships with peers. Teachers, however, and their assistants as well, are very important with respect to separation experiences in the classroom. Adults in a nursery school or kindergarten are, in fact, often viewed as temporary parents. They are, accordingly, turned to again and again for "emotional refueling." Unfortunately, very little of this "refueling" finds its way into stories for young children, particularly stories describing a child's initial school experience. Therefore, *I Am Here: Yo Estoy Aqui* does offer something unique by acknowledging the fact that warm and supportive relationships between children and adults can often play an important role in a young child's early school adjustment.

Separation from Parents for Reasons Not Related to School Activities

Be Good Harry, Ira Sleeps Over, and *First Night Away from Home* all focus attention on the attempt of a young child (or animal) to master an important separation experience away from his or her home or school setting. In *Be Good Harry,* by Mary Chalmers, a very small cat called Harry reluctantly stays with Mrs. Brewster, a well-known and trusted baby-sitter. Harry's mother tells him that she will return in one hour. Although Harry misses his mother and is somewhat unhappy at first, he finally responds to the warmth and friendship of the baby-sitter. Most reassuring of all is the fact that Harry's mother does indeed return soon.

This short, simple story might help very young children grasp the idea that mothers *do* return; that being left with a baby-sitter does not, in any way, represent the irrevocable loss of one's own mother. Young children, however, are not yet ready to fully understand time concepts such as "one hour." Therefore, in reading this story, the adult might de-emphasize the difficult concept of a one-hour time interval and stress the fact that Harry's mother is leaving for just a short time, and that she does indeed return in a little while, just as she had promised.

In *Ira Sleeps Over,* by Bernard Waber, a young boy plans to sleep at a friend's house. At bedtime, on this first night away from home,

Ira has much difficulty getting settled comfortably. Finally, when he is reunited with a favorite toy, a small brown teddy bear, he feels better and soon falls asleep.

It may be comforting for some young readers to see that other children, too, often need a favorite toy to help them face a new experience, and that they are not at all ridiculed by their storybook peers for acknowledging this need.

In *First Night Away from Home,* by Myra B. Brown, Stevie plans to sleep at a friend's house. As he announces this proposed visit to a number of his peers, a variety of separation experiences—staying at a grandparent's house, staying at a hotel, staying overnight at a hospital—are discussed. As in the previous story, Stevie gets settled in his friend's house only to discover that he is highly restless and lonely at bedtime in the strange surroundings. Not until his mother rings the bell and brings his favorite stuffed animal does Stevie feel comfortable and secure enough to fall asleep.

A consideration of some of the realistic feelings, both good and bad, provoked by Stevie's trip might be helpful to a young child who is about to embark on an overnight experience. *First Night Away from Home* can also be a good starting point for a more general discussion between children and adults about staying overnight away from one's parents, and a useful springboard for a consideration of the various feelings, fears, and fantasies such an event is likely to arouse.

Accidental Separation from a Parent or Parent-Figure

Juvenile books describing the experiences of a small child or animal who is temporarily lost could encourage helpful discussion of such experiences with young children. By responding to stories concerning this topic, by sharing ideas and spinning fantasies, children may develop a greater ability to tolerate the experience of becoming momentarily "lost" without undue anxiety.

In *Hello Henry,* by Ilse-Margret Vogel, two young boys, both named Henry, are accidentally separated from their mothers and become lost for a while in a busy supermarket. In *Mike's House,* by Julia L. Sauer, a small boy named Robert busily chases his hat down a windy block only to discover that he can no longer find the building he was about to enter. Later, a friendly policeman helps Robert

find his way back to the local library and his favorite Picture Storybook Hour.

In an even more imaginative and appealing manner, Robert Mc-
Closkey describes what happens on a summer day in Maine when a
little girl named Sal and a little bear cub become separated from their
respective mothers while they are out blueberry picking. There is just
enough suspense in *Blueberries for Sal* to hold a child's eager attention without evoking overwhelming anxiety about a separation experience. By the end of the story, Little Bear and Little Sal are both
happily reunited with their own mothers once again.

For slightly older children, an enchanting folk tale, *My Mother Is
the Most Beautiful Woman in the World,* by Becky Reyher, portrays
the experiences of a young peasant girl who goes from village to village searching for her "lost" mother. Once again, mother and child
are warmly and happily reunited by the end of the story.

Children respond eagerly to stories of this type, often relating their
own experiences about being lost in a store or other public place. Such
books also often generate discussion about what to do when one is
temporarily lost. Most reassuring of all are the scenes reuniting parent
and child at the end of each book.

Used as communication-aids, stories and discussions about temporary or accidental separations may help a young child grow in confidence and begin to understand that becoming unexpectedly separated
from one's parents for a few moments is an experience that can be
met and mastered, too.

Separation from a Well-Liked and Trusted Individual (Friend, Teacher, Therapist, etc.)

Some honest feelings surrounding a necessary separation from a
loved and trusted friend are sensitively portrayed in *Little Bear's
Friend,* by Else H. Minarik. In this story, Little Bear and Emily become very good friends during a summer vacation. Then summer is
over, and it is time for Emily to say good-bye. Little Bear is very sad.
A real-life child currently facing separation from a good friend, separation from a well-loved teacher, or, perhaps, a change from one
therapist to another, may find special meaning in this story. Little
Bear's experience might also provoke some helpful discussion about
separation experiences in general, discussion that may prove valuable
at a later date in coping with separation experiences yet to come.

The separation in *The New Teacher*, by Miriam Cohen, takes place between a group of young children and a much-loved teacher. The first-graders in this story are most unhappy with a necessary change of teachers and very reluctant to accept the expected new-comer. After imagining again and again what then new teacher will be like, the children finally do meet her. The story ends on a rather hopeful note with an indication that a good relationship will probably be established, after a reasonable passage of time, between the reluc-tant children and the new teacher. Here is a story that could have special meaning for young children who must deal with a similar personnel change, perhaps encouraging helpful discussion of the feel-ings and fears involved.

Amos & Boris, by William Steig, also focuses attention on deeply felt separation feelings. Amos, a mouse, and Boris, a whale, became the closest possible friends. As they travelled together, a strong bond was established between them. "They told each other about their lives; their ambitions. They shared their deepest secrets." When circum-stances eventually forced them to separate, Amos and Boris did not forget each other. The close relationship built between them left a lasting effect on each of them.

Young children, who are themselves about to face a required separation from someone important in their own lives, such as a close friend, a well-loved teacher or relative, or perhaps a therapist, may find personal significance in this story. As they become involved in the separations faced by Amos and Boris, they may begin to view their own separation experiences in a new and somewhat clearer light. In addition, they may benefit considerably from an opportunity to dis-cuss selected separation experiences from the storybook world or from their own lives with an understanding and perceptive adult. A consideration of the story *Amos & Boris* might spark such discussion.

Often it takes a long period of time for a child to obtain added emotional strength by sharing a carefully selected book or story with an adult. *Amos & Boris* was in fact used over a nine-month time period by a young boy and a teacher-therapist at the Yale University Child Study Center. Again and again child and therapist focused their attention on various parts of this story, for *Amos & Boris* seemed to furnish an excellent opportunity for the child to talk about the many separations that had already occurred in his own life. In addition, this story helped the boy and therapist to acknowledge the fact that peo-ple often do feel sad when separations must occur. Eventually, thera-pist and child turned their attention to the fact that the boy himself, like Amos and Boris, would soon be facing new experiences and would, perhaps, be better able to deal with separations in the future than he had in the past.

Another type of separation experience is sensitively described in *Benjy's Bird,* by Norma Simon. One spring day Benjy found an injured robin. All through the spring and summer months Benjy cared for the robin and grew very attached to him, too. As the robin grew stronger, he flew away from time to time, but he always returned to Benjy and settled into a small, comfortable nest that Benjy had made for him. When autumn arrived, flocks of birds could be seen overhead flying south. Then Benjy's bird flew away, too. This time he didn't return. Perhaps he flew away with the other birds to a warmer climate, Benjy's mother suggested. Benjy's sadness and his eventual acceptance of the loss of his robin is recounted as a touching, but growth-producing experience, one that can be related to the repeated separations that are apt to occur and recur throughout one's lifetime. Benjy's family help him understand and cope with his loss by offering warmth and support and encouraging him to talk about the incident and about his feelings.

> *"When you are growing up, Benjy," mother said softly, "there are many goodbyes. There are kittens and puppies that go to new homes. There are summers and vacations that go by too fast. There are friends that move to faraway places. There are robins that leave when the days grow cold. You will remember them all, and you will remember your robin."*

With his parents' help, Benjy begins to understand and accept the fact that separations, too, are a part of life.

Separation Feelings and Children's Books: Some Further Suggestions

As indicated previously, the books discussed above have been selected because their use might be helpful in dealing with early separation experiences, and because individuals working with young children might find it beneficial to know that such books are available. The list itself is certainly not an exhaustive one. Other publications relating to the same topic may also be helpful, and, of course, new and possibly valuable material concerning separation experiences may appear from time to time in future juvenile publications.

In a consideration of this topic, however, it does seem important to note that there are in existence today a number of books for young children portraying early separation experiences that cannot be considered helpful from a child development point of view. Typical of such stories are juvenile publications that describe an initial school experience in an unrealistic and nonchildlike manner, such as *The Little School at Cottonwood Corners* (Schick, 1965).[1] In this story, a little girl who is too young to attend school obtains a visitor's pass and spends an entire day, apparently on her own initiative, wandering from classroom to classroom in an unfamiliar school setting. The school itself is presented as an ideal place with ideal children and ideal teachers. No one ever frowns. The child's day is indeed delightful, the only problem being that the story is in no way reminiscent of real experiences with real children. Moreover, children exposed to this book occasionally become disturbed by the stylized drawings and by the fact that none of the children in *The Little School at Cottonwood Corners* has a nose; each child simply has two eyes and a mouth!

Other stories concerning separation experiences that should be avoided, from a child development point of view, portray such experiences in a seemingly flippant and rather casual manner. They seem to suggest that a child can be tricked into easily and cheerfully accepting separation from his or her parents by a series of clever maneuvers on the part of the surrounding adults. Such stories, typified by *Amy Loves Goodbyes* (Gordon, 1966),[2] appear to encourage a denial or distortion of many of the true feelings that are apt to arise in actual parent-child separation experiences, particularly experiences concerning a very young child. Stories of this nature are not likely to help real-life children and their families cope with realistic separation experiences occurring in their own lives.

Similarly, stories about bedtime that totally ridicule a child protagonist should also be avoided when one is selecting a book to help ease or explore bedtime fears. For example, consider *Edie Changes Her Mind* by Johanna Johnston.[3] In this story, the parents outsmart their frightened daughter, who does not want to go to sleep. They do this by dismantling her bed and removing it from her room. Finally

---

[1] Schick, Eleanor. *The Little School at Cottonwood Corners*. New York: Harper & Row, 1965.

[2] Gordon, Selma. *Amy Loves Goodbyes*. Illus. by June Goldsborough. New York: Platt & Munk Co., 1966.

[3] Johnston, Johanna. *Edie Changes Her Mind*. Illus. by Paul Galdone. New York: G. P. Putnam's Sons, 1964.

Edie agrees that she is indeed sleepy, and begs her parents to return her bed. Children's fears should not be ridiculed in this or any other manner. Surely stories that portray parents as clever manipulators cannot offer much help or support for young children at bedtime. Even if such books seem like fun to read, they should not be selected for the purpose of helping a young child cope with his or her own night-time fears.

In addition to the variety of stories described above, it may also be worthwhile to note that there are still some important themes concerning early separation experiences that have, to date, received little, if any, treatment in the juvenile literature available on this topic. For example, a sensitive story emphasizing the development of a *trusting* and *ongoing* relationship between a particular child and teacher would be a welcome addition to the present list of stories portraying initial school experiences. Particularly lacking are stories suggesting the *ongoing* nature of a teacher–child relationship. There is a great emphasis in stories concerning introductory school situations on experiences with other children and with exciting materials, and very little portrayal of a young child's relationship with a warm, supportive kindergarten or nursery-school teacher. It is, however, the teacher who can be most helpful in regard to early school-related separation anxieties. Perhaps, therefore, individuals interested in children's health and child development can encourage greater emphasis on the supportive teacher role in future stories concerning this theme.

Another theme that has not received sufficient treatment in juvenile books concerns the classroom participation of parents whose children are first starting school. At the present time, many nursery schools recommend that a parent remain at school, for gradually decreasing time periods, in order to help a young child become better accustomed to the school setting. When participating in such a plan, parents may remain in the classroom for varying time intervals during the first few days or weeks of the school term, depending upon criteria selected by the teacher.

When inviting parents to initially remain in the classroom, nursery-school teachers are likely to rely upon various criteria, in addition to their own intuitive reactions, in order to select the time that seems most appropriate for separation of a particular parent and child. They will, for example, notice if a child has made an attachment to a teacher and if he or she is able to turn to that teacher for assistance. They will notice if a child is beginning to feel comfortable in the classroom and interested in classroom activities. They will consider how often the child looks for or appears to need the parent and how the child relates to other children. They will, in all likelihood, prefer not to have a young child left too abruptly in a strange classroom nor will they want to become involved in an undue prolongation of a parent's participation in classroom procedures.

Clearly, the presence of parents in selected classrooms at the beginning of a nursery school year is not an unusual phenomenon. Unfortunately, few, if any, children's books illustrate such a gradual separation procedure. In the storybook world, children entering nursery school seldom appear to need the reassuring presence of a parent nearby. It might, however, be helpful to have some perceptive stories available centering around this very procedure. Such stories might portray a child *gradually,* over a period of time, gaining the necessary confidence in himself, in the school situation, and in his own mastery skills, so that eventually he manages quite well without the presence of a parent in the classroom. The appearance of such stories could be a worthwhile addition to publications already existing on the entrance-into-nursery-school theme.

Conclusion

Once again, it must be emphasized that the story materials listed in this chapter are not, of course, a panacea. Children will take what they can from these stories, and from the discussions such stories are likely to initiate, or what they most need or are most able to absorb in relation to their current developmental stages. One hopes, however, that consideration of some of the materials described here will offer children and interested adults a chance to share enjoyable reading experiences and, possibly, an opportunity to achieve emotional growth from the stories selected or, more importantly, from the adult–child interactions such stories are likely to promote.

References

BERGER, A. S. Anxiety in young children. *Young Children,* 1971, *27,* 5–11.
BOWLBY, J. *Separation, anxiety and anger. Attachment and Loss* (vol. II). New York: Basic Books, 1973.

Freud, A. *Normality and pathology in childhood: Assessments of development*. New York: International Universities Press, 1965.

Furman, R. A. Experiences in nursery school consultations. *Young Children*, 1966, *22*, 84–95.

Goodenough, E. W. Fear and anxiety in young children. In E. G. Pitcher (Ed.), *Early childhood education: Eight articles*. Medford, Mass.: Eliot-Pearson School Alumni Association, Tufts University, 1963.

Gross, D. W. On separation and school entrance. *Childhood Education*, 1970, *46*, 250–53.

Kessler, J. W., et al. Separation reactions in young mildly retarded children. *Children*, 1969, *16*, 2–7.

Kimmel, E. A. Can children's books change children's values? *Educational Leadership*, 1970, *28*, 209–14.

Meathenia, P. S. An experience with fear in the lives of children. *Childhood Education*, 1971, *48*, 75–79.

Nagera, H. Sleep and its disturbances approached developmentally. *The Psychoanalytic Study of the Child*, 1966, *21*, 393–447.

Pine, F. On the separation process: universal trends and individual differences. In J. B. McDevitt and C. F. Settlage (Eds.), *Separation-individuation: Essays in honor of Margaret S. Mahler*. New York: International Universities Press, 1971.

Speers, R. W., et al. Recapitulation of separation-individuation processes when the normal three-year-old enters nursery school. In J. B. McDevitt and C. F. Settlage (Eds.), *Separation-individuation: Essays in honor of Margaret S. Mahler*. New York: International Universities Press, 1971.

Webster, J. Using books to reduce the fears of first-grade children. *The Reading Teacher*, 1961, *14*, 159–62.

Juvenile Bibliography: Books Relating to Early Childhood Separation Experiences

Reassuring Stories To Help Counteract Fears of Abandonment

Brown, Margaret W. *The Runaway Bunny*. Illus. by Clement Hurd. New York: Harper & Row, 1942.

Krauss, Ruth. *The Bundle Book*. Illus. by Helen Stone. New York: Harper & Row, 1951.

Schlein, Miriam. *The Way Mothers Are*. Illus. by Joe Lasker. Chicago: Albert Whitman, 1963.

Bedtime Stories

Soothing, Reassuring Stories

BROWN, MARGARET WISE. *Goodnight Moon.* Illus. by Clement Hurd. New York: Harper & Row, 1947.

SCHNEIDER, NINA. *While Susie Sleeps.* Illus. by Dagmar Wilson. Reading, Mass.: Addison-Wesley, 1948.

ZOLOTOW, CHARLOTTE. *Sleepy Book.* Illus. by Vladimir Bobri. New York: Lothrop, Lee & Shepard, 1958.

Stories Portraying Some Inner Concerns Surrounding Bedtime

BECKMAN, KAJ. *Lisa Cannot Sleep.* Illus. by Per Beckman. New York: Franklin Watts, 1969.

BROWN, MYRA B. *Benjy's Blanket.* Illus. by Dorothy Marino. New York: Franklin Watts, 1962.

HOBAN, RUSSELL. *Bedtime for Frances.* Illus. by Garth Williams. New York: Harper & Row, 1960.

KRAUS, ROBERT. *Goodnight Richard Rabbit.* Illus. by N. M. Bodecker. New York: Springfellow Books and E. P. Dutton, 1972.

LIFTON, BETTY JEAN. *Goodnight Orange Monster.* Illus. by Cyndy Szekeres. New York: Atheneum, 1972.

MAYER, MERCER. *There's a Nightmare in My Closet.* New York: Dial Press, 1968.

Stories About Dreams and Dreaming

DE REGNIERS, BEATRICE SCHENK. *A Child's Book of Dreams.* Illus. by Bill Sokol. New York: Harcourt, Brace, 1957.

HELLER, FRIEDRICH C. *The Children's Dream Book.* Illus. by Walter Schmogner. New York: Doubleday, 1972.

LUND, DORIS HEROLD. *Did You Ever Dream?* Illus. by Franklin Luke. New York: Parents' Magazine Press, 1969.

WERSBA, BARBARA. *Amanda Dreaming.* Illus. by Mercer Mayer. New York: Atheneum, 1973.

ZOLOTOW, CHARLOTTE. *I Have a Horse of My Own.* Illus. by Yoko Mitsuhashi. New York: Abelard-Schuman, 1964.

Separation-Type Stories That Might Relate Well to Early School Experiences

BLUE, ROSE. *I Am Here: Yo Estoy Aqui.* Illus. by Moneta Barnett. New York: Franklin Watts, 1971.

BREINBURG, PETRONELLA. *Shawn Goes to School*. Illus. by Errol Lloyd. New York: Thomas Y. Crowell, 1973.

COHEN, MIRIAM. *Will I Have a Friend?* Illus. by Lillian Hoban. New York: Collier, 1967.

KATZOFF, BETTY. *Cathy's First School*. Photographs by Sy Katzoff. New York: Alfred A. Knopf, 1964.

MANNHEIM, GRETE. *The Two Friends*. New York: Alfred A. Knopf, 1968.

STEINER, CHARLOTTE. *I'd Rather Stay with You*. New York: Seabury Press, 1965.

THAYER, JANE. *A Drink for Little Red Diker*. Illus. by W. T. Mars. New York: William Morrow, 1963.

YASHIMA, TARO. *Umbrella*. New York: Viking Press, 1958.

Separation from Parents for Reasons Not Related to School Activities

BROWN, MYRA B. *First Night Away from Home*. Illus. by Dorothy Marino. New York: Franklin Watts, 1960.

CHALMERS, MARY. *Be Good Harry*. New York: Harper & Row, 1967.

WABER, BERNARD. *Ira Sleeps Over*. Boston: Houghton Mifflin, 1972.

Accidental Separation from a Parent or Parent-Figure

MCCLOSKEY, ROBERT. *Blueberries for Sal*. New York: Viking Press, 1948.

REYHER, BECKY. *My Mother Is the Most Beautiful Woman in the World*. Illus. by Ruth Gannett. New York: Lothrop, Lee & Shepard, 1945.

SAUER, JULIA L. *Mike's House*. Illus. by Don Freeman. New York: Viking Press, 1954.

VOGEL, ILSE-MARGRET. *Hello Henry*. New York: Parents' Magazine Press, 1965.

Separation from a Well-Liked and Trusted Individual
(Friend, Teacher, Therapist, etc.)

COHEN, MIRIAM. *The New Teacher*. Illus. by Lillian Hoban. New York: Macmillan, 1972.

MINARIK, ELSE H. *Little Bear's Friend*. Illus. by Maurice Sendak. New York: Harper & Row, 1960.

SIMON, NORMA. *Benjy's Bird*. Illus. by Joe Lasker. Chicago: Albert Whitman, 1965.

STEIG, WILLIAM. *Amos & Boris*. New York: Farrar, Straus & Giroux, 1971.

Hospitalization and Illness

FOR SOME TIME NOW there has been a growing acknowledgment of the fact that the emotional as well as the physical needs of children placed in hospitals demand serious concern. Early research reported by Spitz (1945, 1946) first drew attention to the severe trauma that can be caused by a period of prolonged institutional care for young children. Subsequently, Robertson (1958) alerted professionals to the acute distress that could result from placing young children in hospitals, even for short periods of time, especially when such hospitalization involves separation from the mother. Prugh et al., (1953) reported evidence of numerous emotional disturbances in a group of hospitalized four- to six-year-old children, including the presence of anxiety, phobic and obsessive fear reactions, heightened dependency, misinterpretation of hospital procedures, and persistent concern with mutilation or death. Anna Freud (1952) also delineated various effects of bodily illness on the life of the child, differentiating between effects due to nursing and medical procedures, pain and anxiety, and the emotional demands of the illness itself. Each of these investigators stressed the need for more widespread educational measures and urged the development of preventive techniques to ease the emotional distress of young children in hospitals.

Reports in the psychological, psychiatric, and pediatric literature have continued to indicate a growing concern about the total impact of hospital experiences upon young children. The proceedings of a mental health workshop reported by Shore (1965) urged a reduction in emotional stress among hospitalized children, while Haller, Talbert, and Dombro (1967) offered the suggestion that dangers of psychic trauma when young children undergo minor surgery are considerably greater than dangers of hemorrhage or infection. Similarly, Thesi Bergman and Anna Freud (1966), Gilbert Kliman (1968), and Harold Geist (1965) have all encouraged a spreading movement to "humanize" the hospital care of young children, each offering guidelines to help prevent or reduce the unfortunate amount of emotional damage that has so often become associated with hospitals and young children.

Recent publications emphasize the importance of helping children achieve psychological mastery of an illness or hospital experience as well as physical recovery and rehabilitation and suggest various means of facilitating this process (Petrillo and Sanger, 1972; Oremland and Oremland, 1973). Play equipment is frequently advocated to help children deal with the emotional stresses and strains of hospitalization (Plank, 1971). Less often, the use of selected story material is recommended for this purpose.

This chapter will discuss children's books as useful communicative-aids with ill and hospitalized children. Most of the books discussed have actually been read in hospitals, to ill or recuperating children, by parents, volunteers, students, nurses, teachers, social workers, and psychologists. They are books that often lead to discussions of feelings and fears about hospitalization. They should be presented with ample leisure time for children to raise questions and express feelings. They should be offered in a warm, non-threatening atmosphere with sufficient time and encouragement for children to reflect upon the story material and become involved—in their imaginations —in the fantasies it may evoke.

By using books and stories in this manner, an interested, concerned adult may discover a valuable way to spark a child's imagination, enhance healthy development, create fun, and help the healing process take place.

Imaginative Stories That Portray Hospital Experiences

Stories that show what actually goes on inside a hospital can help make a hospital experience seem less frightening to a young child. Numerous juvenile books of varying quality have been written for this purpose. *Curious George Goes to the Hospital,* by Margret and H. A. Rey, and *Madeline,* by Ludwig Bemelmans, are two of the more imaginative books available involving hospitalization. Both publications have a great deal of child appeal and both can be used to elicit valuable discussion in a hospital pediatric ward.

Curious George Goes to the Hospital, one of a number of well-known and well-loved *Curious George* books, is a frequent favorite with young children. Prepared in collaboration with the Children's Medical Center of Boston, it tells about an engaging monkey who goes to the hospital for emergency surgery. Besides being fun and eliciting an amazing amount of giggles, Curious George introduces children to a number of hospital procedures and techniques. The story acknowledges George's initial fear and bewilderment in the strange surroundings, illustrates his daring but gleeful interruption of hospital routine, and finally demonstrates his recovery and eventual return home. A discussion of George and his hospital adventures, conducted in a sensitive, accepting manner, can be an excellent communicative-aid in a pediatric ward. The following questions have proven useful in eliciting such discussion:

1. How do you think George felt when he had to go to the hospital? Was he frightened?

2. How did you feel when you first came to the hospital? Were you afraid, too?

3. Curious George brought a big red and blue ball along with him to the hospital. Why do you think he brought the ball? Did you bring anything special from home?

4. Some things in the hospital looked scary to George. Does anything in this hospital look scary to you? Which things look scariest?

5. George cried when the nurse gave him a shot, and he cried when he broke the hospital dishes. Do you ever feel like crying here in the hospital? Does crying help? Are you bad or naughty because you cry, or are you simply getting out some of your feelings?

6. How did Curious George feel when it was time to go home? How do you think you will feel when it is time for you to go home?

7. Why did Curious George have to come to the hospital? Why did *you* have to come to the hospital?

With the aid of such questions, Curious George may help unlock some hidden tensions among hospitalized children. Discussion of this book may help children recognize, for example, that others, too, are often fearful or anxious in the hospital, and that crying in response to such fears does not mean that one is a weakling or a sissy. Children often relate illness and hospitalization to punishment. The discussion may also offer opportunities for adults to correct misconceptions of this nature.

Like Curious George, Madeline comes to the hospital for emergency surgery. This is truly a tongue-tickling story, for Madeline comes from a convent "covered with vines," where twelve little girls do almost everything "in two straight lines."

In two straight lines they broke their bread,
and brushed their teeth and went to bed.

And in two straight lines they come to visit Madeline when she is hospitalized for an appendectomy.

Bemelmans portrays a unique feeling of closeness among Madeline and her peers. They are all sad when Madeline goes to the hospital, and they all come eagerly to visit her. Like real-life children, they soon become jealous of the attention and presents Madeline acquires in the hospital and decide, by the end of the story, that they want appendectomies, too!

The positive portrayal of Madeline as a cheerful, daring, amusing, and highly independent youngster makes this book an excellent communicative-aid for hospitalized children. Madeline's illness, it can be noted, was not due to any wrongdoing or evil thought on her part. She simply became ill. Once again, a book discussion can be used to help differentiate illness from punishment in a child's mind.

Attention can also be focused on Madeline's reaction to her scar, a reaction that receives considerable attention in Bemelmans' story. With great pride, Madeline pulls up her pajama top to show off her scar. Emotional responses to operations, however, are apt to vary. Perhaps, like Madeline, one child may view a scar with pride, as a sign that she has survived a difficult and frightening experience. Another child, however, may consider a scar a sign of weakness, an unpleasant reminder that some organ or part of herself was diseased, required removal, and perhaps has been thrown away.

In response to Madeline's story, children can be encouraged to verbalize their own reactions to any surgery they may have experienced. Children who choose to share such information should be listened to in a serious and nonjudgmental manner, for talking about or dramatizing surgery-related concerns can represent important emotional work on a child's part.

The following questions have been helpful in generating discussion about Madeline and her hospital experience:

1. Madeline's friends were almost like sisters to her because they all lived together. How did your sisters or brothers act when you went to the hospital? Do you think they were somewhat jealous of the attention you were receiving? How do you think they will act when you return home?

2. Do you think Madeline was a show-off? How do you think she really felt about her scar? Do you have a scar from surgery?

3. Is Miss Clavell like anyone you know? Does she remind you of anyone?

4. Madeline stared at a crack in the ceiling over her bed until she discovered that it looked like a rabbit. Why do you think she did that? Are you ever bored in the hospital? What do you do when you are bored?

5. Why did Madeline get sick? Why did she need an operation? Why did you have to come to the hospital?

If given a chance, hospitalized children may respond to Madeline in a very special way. Besides being fun, she is, after all, somewhat reassuring, because she does survive her surgical ordeal and, at the same time, she manages to keep her sense of humor, her independence, and her many close friendships in good working order.

Though more realistic than *Madeline* or *Curious George, I Think I Will Go to the Hospital,* by Jean Tamburine, still includes a captivating story line that easily gains the attention of young readers or story-listeners. At first Suzy declares that she will NOT go to the hospital. She will NOT. Later she visits the hospital, meets several staff members, and examines certain hospital equipment. When she returns home, Suzy playacts a hospital experience with her own pets —a duck, a hen and a cat. Then she decides that she is ready to go to the hospital after all. Soon Suzy is shown settling into the hospital to have her tonsils removed, thus illustrating a helpful psychological principle, i.e., acting out a situation in advance of its occurrence can help a child master a potentially threatening situation.

Children about to be hospitalized may benefit, as Suzy did, from playacting their expected hospitalization before it occurs. The opportunity to become familiar with equipment and procedures introduced in this book, in advance of their own hospitalization, can also be beneficial.

Children already in the hospital may choose to imitate Suzy by dramatizing some of their own experiences, such as giving a make-believe shot to a doctor, operating on a doll, or drawing some blood from a puppet. In addition, they may benefit from discussing, with a sensitive adult, some of the issues raised in this story, such as Suzy's initial refusal to go to the hospital. This can lead into discussions of their own hospital-related fears and anxieties along with a consideration of what, if anything, has helped them overcome their fears. Used in this manner, *I Think I Will Go to the Hospital* can facilitate some important verbal interaction between hospitalized children and interested, concerned adults.

Elizabeth Gets Well, by Alfons Weber, also presents realistic hospital information along with a lively, captivating story. The author is an experienced pediatrician and child psychiatrist with a sensitive understanding of young children. Beginning with the very first sentence, "It all started with a stomach ache," he goes on to relate an entire hospital experience from a child's point of view. According to Dr. Weber, this book was written specifically to help diminish fear of the unknown in children who must be hospitalized. There is indeed sufficient information here about various procedures and equipment to help achieve this goal. The book presents, among other activities, a preoperative injection, the operating room, intravenous fluids, allergy tests, the presence of stitches, and the process of taking x-rays. In addition, *Elizabeth Gets Well* is one of the few children's books to illustrate a blood test in color. The needle and bright red blood often draw attention and invite discussion of children's experiences with similar procedures.

Although the realism concerning hospital procedures and routines in *Elizabeth Gets Well* is valuable, the honesty and sensitivity that characterize the entire book may be even more important. For example, in *Elizabeth Gets Well:* (1) The family has to wait some time for the doctor's arrival because he is quite busy. He doesn't suddenly appear like magic and solve everything. (2) At first Elizabeth's brother teases her instead of sympathizing with her plight. (3) After the surgery, discomfort is realistically acknowledged—Elizabeth feels a sharp stab of pain when she tries to move. (4) Elizabeth repeatedly begs for a drink of water, some time after surgery, but she can only have two teaspoonsful of ginger ale—at least for a while. (5) A natural amount of sibling rivalry greets Elizabeth upon her return home.

Children should be given ample opportunity to discuss such topics, particularly from their own point of view, e.g., Did you feel pain after your operation? Were you very thirsty? How do you think your sisters or brothers will act toward you when you return home?

Elizabeth Gets Well was originally published in Switzerland. Some children may be interested in seeing if the hospital equipment shown here is different from standard American equipment. Such interest may also provoke a discussion of hospital equipment in general, with special attention given to children's feelings, fears, and possible misconceptions concerning the intended purpose and use of such equipment.

Some children have used *Elizabeth Gets Well* as an opportunity to talk about the fact that Elizabeth did indeed recover and to seek reassurance that they too will eventually get better.

By sharing reactions to stories of this type, children may discover new ways of coping with the feelings precipitated by their own hospital experiences. Individual concerns and anxieties may be brought to light, and possibly reduced, in the process.

Information-Type Books About Hospitalization

Numerous juvenile publications about hospitalization are presented in a strictly informative manner. Such books often describe, or attempt to describe, a young child's experiences in the hospital. Usually surgery is involved. Before one selects a book of this type, the material should be carefully evaluated. Books that portray hospitalization as a totally happy experience—books that show a child smiling cheerfully after surgery or walking hand-in-hand with a friendly doctor toward the operating room—should be avoided because of the unrealistic information they present and the myths about hospitalization they tend to perpetuate. Books that encourage a child to repress his or her feelings—e.g., to be good or quiet, not to cry and not to be afraid—should also be avoided. Children in the hospital, or about to be hospitalized, need an open acknowledgment and acceptance of their hospital-related fears and anxieties. Instead of being encouraged to repress anxieties, they should be continuously helped to express concerns through play activity and talk. In addition, books that seem to overwhelm children with a multitude of gratuitous facts about hospitalization should be used sparingly, if at all. Though presented in picture-book format, such books frequently are not in keeping with a young child's interest or attention span—e.g., citing information about health insurance, etc. Books of this nature may, in fact, only serve to turn attention *away* from a child's actual fears and anxieties, thus weakening their potential value as communicative-aids.

A carefully chosen information-type book can, however, be helpful both before and during a hospital experience. After returning home, a child who has become accustomed to a particular book in the hospital may want to hear the same story again and again. This should be allowed and even encouraged, as the process of helping children cope with hospitalization should be viewed as a continuous and repetitive one. Books that hold a special meaning for a particular child should, therefore, be made available for as long as they are needed.

The following books offer potentially helpful information about hospital experiences:

What Happens When You Go to the Hospital, by Arthur Shay, is the story of a young girl named Karen who has her tonsils removed. Realistic black-and-white photographs help portray Karen's experiences in the hospital. Anecdotes about the nurses, doctors, and other children are also included. Although this is basically an information-giving book, Karen comes across as a real little girl whose feelings are acknowledged and respected. For the most part, the book portrays a realistic hospital experience, except that more discomfort might have been acknowledged immediately after surgery.

One mother who used this book to help prepare a three-year-old child for a tonsillectomy reported that her daughter had become so familiar with Karen's experiences (and perhaps so comforted by the happy outcome) that she wanted every aspect of her own hospital experience to take place exactly as portrayed in the book. She wanted exactly the same dinner—roast beef, mashed potatoes, milk, and jello —the same nurse, the same bed clothes, and even the same type of identification band. She also noted numerous differences in procedures and was apparently disturbed by them (e.g., "The nurse is supposed to tell me her name"; "Karen kept her toys in bed with her. Why can't I?"). When she returned home from the hospital, she immediately wanted to call Karen on the phone to tell her that *her* operation was over now, too.

Sharing Karen's story with her mother helped this girl cope with her own tonsillectomy. Her expectations once in the hospital, however, clearly highlight the need for parents to prepare children for the fact that their own hospital experiences may differ somewhat from those portrayed in a favorite book.

Bettina Clark's *Pop-Up Going to the Hospital* is frequently found in pediatric wards. This cardboard activity-type book also portrays a tonsillectomy. Though not particularly meritorious in artistic, imaginative, or literary content, it can elicit valuable participation and role-playing on a child's part. The book includes a toy mask, and pictures that pop up; these encourage further imaginative play. Although some procedures are realistically depicted, the author does not sufficiently acknowledge the frightening aspects of hospitalization here. An injection, for example, is described as feeling like a mosquito bite, and the storybook child is shown walking confidently down the corridor with his doctor to the operating room. Other activity-type books about hospitalization, books with greater emphasis on feelings and a more appropriate exclusion of unrealistic information, might be desirable.

A Hospital Story, by Sara Bonnett Stein, one of several "Open Family" books, also deals with a tonsillectomy experience. This book presents information for parents about hospitalization accompanied by a separate text for children. Also included are large, realistic photographs taken at home and at the hospital.

The greatest value of *A Hospital Story* is its attempt to bring feelings, often hidden or denied, out into the open. "It is quite all right for a child to be angry, if that is how he feels," the book reminds parents. Jill, the little girl in this book, is encouraged, at first, to express some of her inner concerns regarding an imminent hospital experience in repeated doll play, drawings, and talks with her mother. These activities help her become emotionally ready for the real experience. Parents are urged to look for and recognize misconceptions about illness, not to make unrealistic promises to a child about what to expect in the hospital, and to obtain, and share with an-about-to-be-hospitalized child, accurate information about hospital settings and routines.

Jill successfully undergoes a tonsillectomy. Those aspects of a hospital experience most likely to disturb a young child are not glossed over here. Jill does not like "hospital clothes, blood tests, making pee-pee in a bottle, and shots." In the text for parents, much discussion is centered on Jill's concern about her own body integrity and her concern about separation from her parents.

Jill survives the surgery well. When she returns home she eats red

Jell-o and shouts in a very loud voice. Parents are then advised about tantrums, sleeping difficulties, and a heightened need for reassurance, behavior that may become evident shortly after a hospital experience. The last picture shows Jill swinging happily on a park swing, so that children can recognize that Jill is indeed well again.

One of the few concerns that has been expressed regarding *A Hospital Story* is the possibility that perhaps too much information about hospitalization is offered here, much of it presented in a cautionary voice. Parents should not be intimidated by the nature of this book—e.g., the psychological orientation of the text and the many advisory statements directed toward parents. They should, instead, use the material as it seems most suitable in regard to their own child's needs and their own ability to share such information. Approached in this manner, *A Hospital Story* can best serve its primary purpose of keeping lines of communication open between children and adults about a hospital experience.

A Hospital Story is mainly oriented toward parents and children. It could, however, also be used as a valuable resource guide for hospital staff and volunteers, helping them to become more familiar with the inner thoughts, fears, and misconceptions that may concern a young, hospitalized child.

Jeff's Hospital Book, by Harriet Sobol, also portrays an actual hospital stay. Simple text and sensitive photographs describe the experiences of a young boy undergoing eye surgery. The acknowledgment of fears and feelings combined with accurate hospital information make this a highly useful book. In addition, the realistic portrayal of an eye operation is particularly valuable since so many hospital storybooks concentrate on tonsillectomies.

Most of the strictly information-type books about hospitalization use large realistic photographs. Some children, however, prefer bright, simple illustrations that do not, for example, bring them into contact with a "real-life" child about to undergo surgery. Illustrations, instead of photographs, often present children a greater opportunity to weave their own fantasies around the happenings suggested in a story. Simon Lesser (1957) calls this process "analogizing" and explains that we can obtain the greatest benefit possible from a literary experience by imaginatively putting ourselves into a story. Photographs sometimes inhibit this process, for as one child stated, "There already is a *real* little girl in that story."

Going into Hospital, by Althea, might, therefore, be an excellent book for three- to five-year-olds about to face hospitalization. This small picture book, published in England, includes clear, simple illustrations with much child appeal. The inside cover—to be read to or by a child—suggests:

> *If you are ill*
> *or have an accident,*
> *you may need to go into hospital,*
> *so they can*
> *make you better.*
>
> *This book tells you*
> *what it is like*
> *when you are there.*

Going into Hospital then introduces a number of children who have come to the hospital for various reasons. Pain and discomfort are not denied, but the general feeling is that each child masters and manages the situation quite well, and that the reader will, too, if he or she has to go to the hospital. Both male and female doctors are shown. The book is brief and simple enough to be read at one sitting. It can, in fact, be read again and again, each time generating different questions and encouraging the elaboration of different details. In addition to sharing the story with an adult, *Going into Hospital* can become an important personal possession for a young hospitalized child. If allowed to keep this small paperback book, a child can return to it often, whenever the need or desire to do so arises, both in and out of the hospital.

Many hospitals have created their own books or pamphlets to acquaint children with a hospital setting or with specific hospital procedures. For example, *Michael's Heart Test* and *Margaret's Heart Operation,* two pamphlets prepared at the Children's Hospital of Philadelphia, offer valuable information concerning specific cardiac procedures (catheterization and heart surgery). Both can be adapted for use with children undergoing similar procedures at other hospitals. For slightly older children, a booklet entitled *A Letter to Blackie,* distributed to patients at the Department of Pediatrics and Contagious Diseases at Cleveland Metropolitan General Hospital, offers excellent hospital-prepared material. This booklet describes what one youngster experienced, thought, and feared about his own surgery and how he confided this information, by letter, to his dog, Blackie. Written by Marlene Ritchie, the booklet is included, in its entirety, in Emma Plank's *Working with Children in Hospitals* (1971).

Most juvenile books about hospitalization portray surgery. Such books must be evaluated carefully in relation to a particular child's needs. The idea of someone cutting into his or her body can be very frightening to a young child. Fantasies of being attacked, over-whelmed, or mutilated may arise or be reactivated by thoughts of surgery. If a hospitalized child is *not* expected to undergo surgery, books describing operations may simply exaggerate existing fears or generate new anxieties. On the other hand, a child facing complex surgery and lengthy recuperation may not gain much emotional sup-port from a book portraying minor surgery followed by immediate recovery. The child may feel instead that he has been tricked.

Clearly more books portraying the experiences of children in the hospital for reasons other than surgery—such as for diagnostic pur-poses or for chronic illnesses—are needed. Also needed are more books describing the experiences of children undergoing surgery more complicated than a tonsillectomy.

A carefully selected information-type book about the hospital can be a valuable aid in the preparation of young children for hospitaliza-tion. If an appropriate book cannot be found for a particular child or situation, interested hospital staff, mental health professionals, and parents might consider creating their own material, based upon their own experiences with children in hospitals. Helping children cope with hospitalization and illness is an ongoing, repetitive process. Find-ing or creating juvenile books to assist children in gaining emotional mastery of a hospital experience can be one way of enhancing this process.

Books Portraying Experiences and Emotions That May Have Special Meaning for the Hospitalized Child

In addition to books about hospitalization and hospital proce-dures, books on other topics often have special significance for the hospitalized child.

A child in the hospital is in a highly vulnerable position. He or she may experience frightening feelings such as separation anxieties, loneliness, apathy, loss of self-esteem, and concern about body image and integrity. A generalized feeling of weakness or dependency, ac-companied by regression to more infantile modes of behavior, may become evident. Anger, suspicion, and a fear of abandonment by those the child needs and loves the most may also exist.

The books discussed in this section speak directly and/or symbolically to such feelings. By using them wisely, an adult may be able to facilitate the healing process so that a hospitalized child who is recovering physically can also be helped to grow emotionally.

Separation Feelings and the Hospitalized Child

One of the most helpful books for hospitalized children is not about hospitalization at all. *Ira Sleeps Over,* by Bernard Waber, describes a child's overnight visit to a friend's house, focusing attention on the young boy's uncertainties when bedtime arrives. Finally, with the help of a favorite toy, Ira manages to master his doubts and fears about sleeping away from home.

For many children, separation from parents may be the most upsetting aspect of a hospital experience. For toddlers and preschool-aged children the fears aroused by such separations, and the incapacity to understand the reality of the situation, can cause great distress. A child may, for example, anticipate permanent loss of his or her parents when temporarily separated from them, or interpret the disappearance of a parent as punishment for "being bad." Robertson (1953) and Bowlby (1961), among others, have observed sequences of *protest, despair,* and *detachment* as characteristic of young children who have been separated from their parents and placed in institutional settings. Numerous emotional repercussions have also been observed in future development following such experiences. Arrangements for a parent to remain with an infant or toddler may, therefore, be a crucial factor in the child's eventual ability to cope with, and master, a hospital experience. At that young age, the value of a storybook presentation rapidly pales next to the importance of a parent's presence.

For older preschool and primary-grade children, however, books portraying parent-child separation experiences reportedly have been helpful before, during, and even after a child's hospital stay. Books like Bernard Waber's *Ira Sleeps Over,* Myra Brown's *First Night Away from Home,* and Charlotte Steiner's *I'd Rather Stay with You* all offer excellent opportunities for children and adults to consider together some of the fears, feelings, and misconceptions that a required separation between parents and children may generate. (These books are discussed in Chapter II.) In addition, a sensitive anthropomorphic interpretation of the parent-child separation theme appears in *The Little Brown Gazelle* by Gail Barclay. Here, a small gazelle follows his mother's instructions and waits in the jungle for her return. Numerous incidents frighten him while his mother is away. Like the gazelle, hospitalized children, too, may have to survive various ordeals without a parent's reassuring presence. Frequently, a child in the hospital will focus attention on the happy ending in this book—the satisfying reunion between the gazelle and its mother sometimes sparking a sensation of hope in a child awaiting his or her own parent's visit.

Stories showing brief, even momentary, separations between parents and children can also be useful in the hospital. (A discussion of books on this theme appears in Chapter II.) *The Bundle Book,* by Ruth Krauss, and *The Runaway Bunny,* by Margaret Wise Brown, are both excellent choices to help counteract a fear of abandonment in the hospitalized child.

Children may find personal consolation in reading or looking at such books themselves, or they may prefer to share them with interested, understanding adults. In either case, books of this type can prove valuable by helping children realize that they, too, like the storybook characters, will be reunited with their parents after each temporary separation.

Nighttime in the Hospital

Nighttime in the hospital can be particularly frightening to young children. Unusual noises, approaching footsteps, and unexpected lights can all serve to exacerbate a child's understandable fear in strange surroundings.

To help counteract fears and anxieties at night, books like *Goodnight Moon,* by Margaret Wise Brown, and *Sleepy Book,* by Charlotte Zolotow, can be used with preschool-aged children.

Goodnight Richard Rabbit, by Robert Kraus, and *Bedtime for Frances,* by Russell Hoban, are good selections for older children who have already gained an understanding of the difference between reality and fantasy. Each of these books portrays a storybook character who imagines numerous fearful happenings at bedtime. As children join in the fantasies depicted here—and create new fantasies in response to the story material—they may become better able to deal with and master their own nighttime fears.

Other books, such as *While Susie Sleeps,* by Nina Schneider, can be used to help reassure hospitalized children that someone is alert and caring for them during the night.

Anxieties associated with hospitalization may initiate an increasing number of disturbing dreams in young children. *Did You Ever Dream?*, by Doris Lund, and *Amanda Dreaming*, by Barbara Wersba, are both excellent books to help children and adults talk about dream sensations and the feelings associated with them. Further discussion of books relating to nighttime fears and dreaming can be found in Chapter II.

In addition, stories that help children interpret the meaning of unexpected sounds can provide valuable information and reassurance regarding nighttime disturbances in the hospital. A series of books by Margaret Wise Brown—including, among others, *The Quiet Noisy Book, The Indoor Noisy Book, The Winter Noisy Book,* and *The Summer Noisy Book*—are excellent choices here. These books describe the experiences of a small dog named Muffin who likes to guess the origin and meaning of various noises. In *The Quiet Noisy Book,* Muffin is awakened by a very quiet noise! "Was it an ant crawling?" "Was it a mouse sighing?"

> *Was it an*
> *ELEPHANT*
> *tiptoeing*
> *down*
> *stairs?*

Similarly helpful in focusing attention on fear-inducing noises are *Do You Hear What I Hear?*, by Helen Borten, *Too Much Noise,* by Ann McGovern, and *What's in the Dark?*, by Carl Memling.

Story discussions in the hospital may help some children learn that they are not alone in their nighttime fears. Children may also discover that opportunities to talk about frightening occurrences or thoughts in a nonthreatening storybook atmosphere can actually reduce the amount of fear experienced.

Self-Esteem and the Hospitalized Child

The hospitalized child can easily regress to more passive and dependent levels of development. Much attention of necessity may be focused on his general weakness and need for help. He may require assistance with eating, bathing, dressing, and bathroom activities, regardless of his previous accomplishments in these areas. It can be particularly threatening to be forced to give up newly-acquired and, therefore, very precious achievements in such areas. The hospitalized child may have to submit, often uncomprehendingly, to various un-familiar, and possibly humiliating, medical procedures. Often he will begin to feel more and more babyish and helpless in the hospital. Carefully selected books can help counteract such feelings by directing (or redirecting) attention to a child's own strengths and abilities.

The Five Chinese Brothers, by Claire Bishop and Kurt Wiese, *Whistle for Willie,* by Ezra Jack Keats, and *Flip,* by Wesley Dennis, all portray storybook characters with unusual skills. Books like these can lead easily into questions such as, "Can you tell me about something wonderful you can do?"—thus generating discussion of a child's unique abilities (real or imagined) rather than his illness or weakness. The following questions can be helpful in encouraging such discussion:

For *Whistle for Willie*
1. Peter wished very much that he could whistle. Finally, he learned how to do it. Did you ever learn to do something special? Was it difficult to learn?
2. What other things are you especially good at doing?
3. Is there something else that you would like to learn how to do? Do you think you will learn some day?

For *The Five Chinese Brothers*
1. Each of the five Chinese brothers could do something very special. Can you remember what they could do?
2. What things are you especially good at doing?
3. How do you feel when you do these things?
4. What can you do that makes you feel proudest of all?

For *Flip*
1. More than anything else in the world, Flip wanted to be able to jump over the brook. What kind of things would you most like to be able to do? What special things can you do right now?
2. Did Flip really need magic wings to jump over the brook?
3. Did you ever wish that you could do something and then discover that you really *could* do it? How did you feel then?

Discussions of this nature, if handled in a sensitive, accepting manner, can help strengthen self-esteem and pride at a time when such attributes are particularly vulnerable to disparagement and despair.

Other books that have been used successfully to encourage discussion of personal skills and accomplishments among hospitalized children include *Crow Boy,* by Taro Yashima, and *One Little Girl,* by Joan Fassler. Both books suggest that what a child accomplishes may be less important emotionally than how the child actually feels about what he or she is doing.

The Carrot Seed, by Ruth Krauss, and *The Little Red Lighthouse and the Great Gray Bridge,* by Hildegarde Swift and Lynd Ward, both portray storybook characters whose activities result in considerable enhancement of their own self-esteem. Such books, too, can often engage children in thoughts or fantasies that affect their own feelings of self-worth in a positive manner.

Maintaining a Sense of Independence and Autonomy

Besides encouraging a possible loss of self-esteem, the fact that a child must submit helplessly to so many activities and procedures in the hospital often weakens a hard-won sense of autonomy. A hospitalized child who makes a reasonable protest in the face of emotionally unreasonable demands might be viewed as a child who is struggling to maintain mental health rather than one deliberately choosing to be a difficult patient. Stories that stress independent thought and action are helpful in reminding children in the hospital that there are many things they can still do their own way—they still possess some amount of control over their own lives, if not always in reality, surely in their imaginations.

No Roses for Harry, by Gene Zion, is an excellent choice to help strengthen a hospitalized child's sense of control over his or her own destiny. Harry, an independent and self-respecting dog, receives a sweater handknitted by Grandma and decorated with full-blown roses. It is not at all what Harry chooses to wear, so he uses all his ingenuity to see that the sweater disappears and is replaced by one more suitable to his own taste and self-image. Hospitalized children too may feel emotionally more comfortable by exchanging routine hospital clothes for at least *some* clothing of their own selection. Harry may give them courage to do just that.

The Tale of Peter Rabbit, by Beatrix Potter, and *The Story about Ping,* by Marjorie Flack and Kurt Wiese, both portray childlike protagonists who persist in doing things their own way, often in contradiction to an adult's cautionary proscription. Peter receives comfort and camomile tea to help him relax after his exciting, hairraising adventure in Mister McGregor's cabbage patch, while Ping gets a slap on the bottom for having explored the Yangtze River instead of returning to the family's houseboat at the proper time. Their independent escapades, however, apparently cause no great harm or loss of love.

Little Bear, a well-loved juvenile book character introduced by Else Minarik, engages in a sprightly dialogue with his mother in which he also adamantly maintains his sense of independence and autonomy —up to a point.

Reflecting upon such stories can help spark, once again, a child's own desire for self-determination. He may deal with such feelings through imagination and fantasy-life, or he may attempt to become more independent himself, in reality. In either case, he may become less passive and submissive in the hospital and possibly a little more difficult for hospital staff to handle. A hospitalized child may become more comfortable with himself, however, and feel less disturbed by his hospital experiences, once he has discovered that Harry, an independent dog, Peter Rabbit, Ping, and Little Bear are all cheering him on.

Encouraging an Open, Honest Expression of Feelings

An opportunity for the verbalization of feelings has often been singled out as one of the most successful ameliorative measures available in dealing with the psychological response to hospitalization. Gilbert Kliman (1968), among others, has noted that overcontrol of fear, suppression, denial and avoidance of anxiety-related topics are all measures which may "collapse with a bang" for the hospitalized child. Instead, he suggests that children in hospitals urgently need an acceptance and open acknowledgment of their fears, as well as numerous opportunities to express their concerns in play activity and talk. Similarly, Sula Wolff (1969) reports research from England indicating that encouragement to talk about fears and worries can lead to better long-term adaptation to illness for hospitalized children. The most helpful intervention in the hospital in support of emotional health, Wolff suggests, is to let children talk rather than to give them explanations and instructions.

In keeping with this view, *The Boy with a Problem*, by Joan Fassler, has been used successfully to encourage the expression of feelings among hospitalized children. The book tells about a boy named Johnny who is deeply troubled about a problem. The story concentrates on Johnny's feelings, never revealing the nature of his problem. Johnny doesn't begin to feel better until his friend, Peter, spends considerable time listening to him in a serious, accepting, and noninterrupting manner.

In a recent pilot project, children in the hospital were asked to guess what Johnny's problem might have been. Numerous responses contained medical or physical connotations, thereby indicating the children's ability to identify with a storybook character and their propensity to extend story material, in their imaginations, to suit their own needs. Some ideas concerning the nature of Johnny's problem included: He needed a shot; He has a sore throat; He was scared, afraid that someone would hurt him; Maybe something was stuck in his throat; He was scared his parents were going to send him away forever.

Like Johnny, hospitalized children will benefit optimally from shared story experiences if their own reactions to such stories are listened to carefully and respectfully. Questions such as the following can be used to encourage a potentially helpful discussion of *The Boy with a Problem:*

1. What do you think Johnny's problem was?

2. Why do you think Johnny didn't feel much like eating or playing at the beginning of this story? Do you ever feel that way when something is bothering you?

3. Why do you think Johnny felt a little better after he talked to his friend?

4. Do you have someone who listens to you?

5. How does it make you feel when someone listens to your problems? Does it help?

6. How does it make you feel when no one listens to your problems? What do you do then?

7. Are you a good listener?

In addition, children may enjoy dramatizing this story, playing either the role of the boy with the problem or the role of Peter, a friend who takes the time to listen. An adult may invite interested children to draw their own illustrations in response to this story (e.g., pictures showing how Johnny felt when he was disturbed; pictures showing Johnny when he began to feel better; and pictures illustrating various possibilities as to what Johnny's problems might have been).

Other books that support and encourage the expression of feelings include *Pavo and the Princess,* by Evaline Ness, the story of a princess who learns how to cry; *Youngest One,* by Taro Yashima, the story of a small Japanese boy who hides behind his mother's skirt because of his inability to communicate a desire for friendship; and *The Terrible Thing That Happened at Our House,* by Marge Blaine, the story of a young girl who finally airs some pent-up feelings and gains her parent's attention and respect in the process.

Books that focus attention on specific emotions can also be used to help children express feelings. Books portraying loneliness, anger, and fear, for example, sometimes give hospitalized children the courage needed to talk about similar feelings on their own part.

Loneliness is beautifully depicted in the story *Maxie,* by Mildred Kantrowitz. Although this story is about an elderly woman, hospitalized children often respond sensitively to Maxie. They seem to understand and sympathize with her plight, for they can imagine only too well what it is like to feel frightened and alone and possibly separated from those who care the most. Questions such as, "Do you ever feel like Maxie?" can evoke a healthy sharing of feelings in a hospital pediatric ward.

Maxie felt better when she discovered that her friends truly needed and loved her. Hospitalized children can talk about people at home, friends, and relatives who need and love them, too. Like Maxie, they may discover that actually they are not as "alone," either in the hospital or at home, as they had feared.

A group discussion of this book can, by its very nature, encourage human interaction, thus providing an initial means of counteracting loneliness in the hospital. Questions like the following can help initiate such discussion:

1. Have you ever felt like Maxie?

2. Maxie felt better when she discovered her neighbors really needed and loved her. Who are the people who most need and love you?

3. Are you sometimes lonely in the hospital? What do you do then?

4. Do you know anyone lonely—anyone like Maxie?

Nannabah's Friend, by Mary Perrine, and *The Lonely Doll,* by Dare Wright, also portray loneliness. Both books can have a special meaning for children coping with long, lonely hours in the hospital or for those facing required separations from family and friends.

Anger, even rage, are not uncommon emotions among hospitalized children. Children may be angry at their parents for allowing their illness or hospitalization to take place or for leaving them in strange and frightening surroundings. Pain and the indignities inflicted upon them in the hospital (real or imagined) may generate further anger. Motor restraint, in particular, is often associated with heightened aggressive feelings.

One valuable way to encourage hospitalized children to express such feelings and overcome associated inner stress is through play activities—dolls, teddy bears, and puppets often passively endure whatever the child has been exposed to in the hospital. Books, too, can become valuable tools for acknowledging and exploring angry and aggressive feelings with hospitalized children.

The Temper Tantrum Book, by Edna Preston, describes the situations that make each of a series of animals angry. Sharing this book with an understanding adult can lead naturally into talk about things that make a child angry, too.

I Was So Mad! by Norma Simon, shows various events that evoke anger and frustration in children's lives. This book clearly acknowledges a child's right to be angry. Feelings are not mocked or denied; instead, the children portrayed are encouraged to deal with their anger in ways acceptable to themselves and to others.

Alexander and the Terrible, Horrible, No Good, Very Bad Day, by Judith Viorst, also focuses attention on anger and frustration. Alexander *knew* it was going to be a miserable day from the moment he woke up with gum in his hair. He was right. Everything went wrong at home and at school. He thought of moving to Australia, but his mother told him that some days are like that—even in Australia.

Simple, brief questions can help children relate Alexander's experiences to similar occurrences in their own lives:

1. When you have a bad day, what makes it bad for you?

2. Did any of the things that happened in this story ever happen to you? How did you feel then? What did you do?

3. What do you think the next day (tomorrow) will be like for Alexander? How about for you?

Another book useful for generating discussion of angry feelings in the hospital is Maurice Sendak's *Where the Wild Things Are.* After a dispute with his mother, Max is sent to his room without supper. In his imagination, he sails off to a land of wild things and meets fantastic monsters, each of whom he eventually conquers and controls. When his angry feelings are spent, Max returns home and finds his supper still hot, waiting for him.

Where the Wild Things Are offers children permission to talk about angry and aggressive feelings. It also offers adults an opportunity to acknowledge that such feelings *do* exist and to suggest that anger can be expressed and dealt with in various suitable ways. Particularly valuable here is the fact that Max masters his angry feelings and that his temporary anger does not irreparably destroy his relationship with his mother.

In response to Max's story, hospitalized children may want to talk about their own experiences with anger and frustration, often creating excellent opportunities for sensitive adults to help them learn how to deal successfully with such feelings. Preschool-aged children, however, who do not understand the difference between fantasy and reality, may find Sendak's monsters truly frightening. The book, therefore, is most suitable for use with children who can share Max's fantasy without the arousal of undue anxiety.

Fear is another common emotion in the hospital. Children may fear the strange surroundings and equipment, hospital procedures and techniques, and punishment or desertion by their loved ones. They may fear being attacked or mutilated or held captive in the hospital. They may fear the unknown and worry about what will happen next. They may fear rejection, ridicule, and imaginary terrors of many sorts. Whether their fears can be objectively justified or not, their emotions are very real.

Whenever possible, adults should encourage children to talk about things they fear. Once again, a carefully selected book can serve as a valuable catalyst for such discussion. In addition to information-type books about hospitalization, which can be useful in dispelling fear, books about fear per se can have special meaning in the hospital. *Scaredy Cat,* by Phyllis Krasilovsky, introduces a little black kitten who is afraid of many things. As they imitate the kitten, or dramatize the story, children often describe things that frighten them in the hospital. For somewhat older children, *Chipmunk in the Forest,* by Eleanor Clymer, portrays an Indian boy who is afraid of the forest and all that it symbolizes. *The Bears on Hemlock Mountain,* by Alice Dalgliesh, tells the story of a boy who manages to master his fear of crossing a certain mountain. Books about nighttime often portray fears too, frequently focusing attention on a child's inner fears and fantasies at bedtime. In addition, books portraying temporary separation experiences can be useful in counteracting fears engendered by required parent-child separations in the hospital.

Discussion based on books portraying fear can help interested, sensitive adults learn more about the kinds of situations, both real and imaginary, that are apt to create fear in a hospitalized child. Children, in turn, may benefit emotionally by opportunities to share and explore fears of their own in the nonthreatening situation of a storybook discussion. By becoming personally involved in discussions of this nature, children may discover an important psychological truth—that fears openly acknowledged and discussed often lose some of their terrorizing quality.

Books To Help Build Personal Courage

My Mother Is the Most Beautiful Woman in the World, a Russian folktale by Becky Reyher, was read to *B*, a ten-year-old, hospitalized girl whose face had been scarred by repeated operations. Hospital staff reported that the child had been withdrawn and did not mix with other children. In response to questions about the scars on her face, *B* remained silent.

The story selected for *B* is about a young girl in Russia who is lost. She goes from village to village asking the inhabitants if they have seen her mother. Upon being asked to describe her mother, the girl repeatedly states, "She is the most beautiful woman in the world!" At last mother and child are reunited. Clearly the rather stout, simple mother is not a physically attractive woman. The joy of their reunion, however, reaffirms the truth that she *is* beautiful in her daughter's eyes.

This story was shared by *B* and a hospital volunteer on several occasions. Staff reported that *B* was unusually attentive at each reading, which greatly surprised them since the story is a comparatively long one. Such attention is sometimes a clue to personal significance. Simon Lesser (1957), among others, has noted that any story which deeply absorbs our attention satisfies some of our needs.

In response to this story, *B* first began to talk about her grandmother, who she said always seemed pretty to *her* but probably did not seem pretty to others. She did not directly speak about her own facial disfigurement.

After several readings of the story, *B* began to interact with other children. Staff reported that she responded for the first time to questions about her scar. Her doctor commented on her changed attitude, noting that *B* had become much more outgoing in the past few days. *B* asked for this story repeatedly each time the volunteer visited her floor. Finally, she asked permission to keep the book for a while.

Apparently, *B*'s response to the story, and her response to the volunteer as well, helped her discover a personal meaning in an old folktale, thereby suggesting the rich possibilities for emotional growth inherent in a story–child–adult interaction experience.

Other books have also affected hospitalized children in a personally significant manner. *Changes, Changes*, by Pat Hutchins, a wordless picture book that includes large, bright illustrations of fire, helped one young boy, recovering from serious burns talk for the first time about fire. *Crooked Colt*, by Clarence Anderson, the story of a colt whose legs were very, very weak but eventually grew strong, helped another boy express some honest reactions to required rehabilitative exercise.

Occasionally a story–child–adult interaction experience seems to promote insight, reduce anxiety, and nourish hope in a hospitalized child. Bearing witness to such an occurrence helps strengthen the belief that children's books, used as vehicles for communication, can and do help children grow.

Books Describing a Visit to a Doctor's or Dentist's Office

A movement away from two outstanding flaws in books describing visits to a doctor's or dentist's office has recently taken place. For a long time such visits were portrayed for the most part as pleasing ones, illustrated by calmly acquiescing children and constantly smiling medical personnel; also, sexism appeared to be more rampant here than in any other area of the children's book field. *A Visit to the Dentist* (Garn, 1959)[1] serves to illustrate both shortcomings. Here a boy and girl each climb cheerfully into the dentist's chair. Wide grins are offered in anticipation of drilling. No indication of fear, pain, or discomfort is offered. The dentist discusses the possibility of the young boy becoming a dentist himself someday. Then he suggests that the girl might look forward to becoming a dental assistant. Both children

[1] Garn, Bernard. *A Visit to the Dentist*. Illus. by Arthur Krusz. New York: Grosset & Dunlap, 1959.

leave happily with medals for good behavior and bright new tooth-brushes.

In contrast, two of the Menninger Clinic Series of juvenile books, *My Friend the Doctor* and *My Friend the Dentist,* both by Jane Watson, do raise several psychologically sound points and do portray at least some honest feelings. Suggestions are offered to help parents talk about illness or anticipate doctor or dentist visits with young children. *My Friend the Doctor* also describes a doctor's visit to an ill child at home. Both books are intended for preschool-aged children and both emphasize how a doctor or dentist helps keep a child well. These books offer important information for parents and children to share together. Even here, however, there is a slight overemphasis on the pleasantness of the situation, for the terms, "My friend the doctor," and "My friend the dentist," are somewhat overused. Parents may want to point out that doctors and dentists are human too, and may not *always* feel or act friendly.

Tommy Goes to the Doctor, by Gunilla Wolde, also presents a preschooler's visit to the doctor. Simple explanations are offered for each procedure undertaken. His mother's reassuring presence during the entire visit helps Tommy master the situation without undue anxiety. *Tommy Goes to the Doctor* is one of the first picture books to portray the doctor as a woman. Prior to this small publication, storybook doctors have almost always been depicted as men. When nursery-school children exposed to this book decide to "play doctor," girls often request the doctor role.

Harlow Rockwell's *My Doctor* also describes a child's visit to a doctor who happens to be a woman. The stress here is on simple, clear pictures and brief descriptions of procedures and equipment. Feelings are not expressed. Parents may be able to extend the value of this publication by presenting children with opportunities to express feelings and concerns about doctor visits and by encouraging them to raise any questions that the pictures or text may inspire.

Dental procedures and equipment are similarly explained by Rockwell in a picture book entitled *My Dentist.* Soft illustrations, large print, and brief, simple descriptions help introduce the dentist and his tools to young children. Like *My Doctor,* this book, too, can be used both as a source of information and as a stimulus for further discussion.

Mister Rogers Talks About . . . , by Fred Rogers, includes a brief section on going to the doctor. Of special interest here is an acknowl-

edgment of the child's possible reaction to medical procedures. For example, when a stethoscope is used, the doctor reassures the child that nobody—not even a doctor—can see or hear what the child is thinking. Realistic photographs, taken in a doctor's office, help describe the visit.

At a more advanced level, Vicki Cobb's *How the Doctor Knows You're Fine* describes, in detail, exactly what the doctor does during a physical check-up and explains what various parts of an examination can reveal about an individual's health. The emphasis here is scientific and informative.

One of the few imaginative picture books describing a visit to a doctor's office is *Doctor Rabbit* by Jan Wahl. This appealing story introduces a warm, endearing doctor from the animal kingdom. Owl comes to see him with a broken wing; Cricket comes with a high fever; Squirrel arrives with a sore throat. Doctor Rabbit cares for them all. Then one day he gets sick himself and his patients take care of *him*. This is an excellent book to show children that doctors are human, not gods. Frequently, it initiates imaginative doctor-play among young children, often encouraging them to assume active rather than passive roles regarding illness.

Doctor Rabbit appears to be the best liked and most caring physician in the picture book field. On the walls of his waiting room he hung poems for his patients to read. When babies were about to be born, he raced through the forest like lightning. Even when snow and ice covered the ground, he bundled up and faithfully visited the ill. Often, he stayed up late and studied enormous books to help his patients get well.

When asked if their own doctors were like Doctor Rabbit, in any way at all, young hospitalized children gave interesting responses:

No, because my doctor is not a rabbit.
No, because real doctors don't get sick.
No—Doctor Rabbit lived in an office. Real doctors live in the hospital.
Yes, when my doctor is in a good mood, he talks to me and makes up poems.

Books describing doctor/dentist visits can be useful communicative-aids for parents and children, offering a familiar and comfortable framework within which to talk about illness and health. Fortunately, newer books on this topic are less stilted and artificial in tone than previous publications. Children and parents will therefore be able to select those that best suit their own needs—books they can turn to frequently, for information and reassurance, throughout the early years of childhood.

Stories About Illness or Pain in General

Juvenile books, like real-life children, depict various reactions to illness. *A Day Off*, by Tobi Tobias, tells about a boy who is mildly sick and enjoys a day home from school. He wants to be sick enough to be pampered and allowed special privileges but not sick enough to require medicine or a doctor. *Tell Me a Mitzi*, by Lore Segal, presents three humorous family stories, one of which portrays the whole family suffering from the sniffles—adults as well as children becoming whiney and restless in the process. Such books often motivate children to talk about their own responses to illness.

I Want Mama, by Marjorie Sharmat, tells about a small girl struggling to cope with her mother's illness and hospitalization, while *Benjie on His Own*, by Joan Lexau, describes a boy's experiences and concerns when his grandmother becomes ill and is taken by ambulance to the hospital. Both books focus attention on the feelings and fears that an illness in the family may generate. They offer interested, concerned adults an excellent opportunity to reassure children once again that illness is not a punishment for any wrongdoing or evil thought on a child's part. They also help focus attention on the changes in a child's life an illness in the family may create.

Pain is frequently charged with considerable psychic meaning for a young child. Anna Freud, for example, points out that children are apt to attribute to outside or internalized agencies whatever painful process occurs within the body or whatever hurt happens to the body (accidental hurts, falls, knocks, cuts, abrasions, etc.). Thus, in his or her own interpretation, a child in pain is often "a child maltreated, harmed, punished, persecuted, threatened by annihilation" (Freud, 1952, p. 76).

In addition to books about hospitalization and illness, which may portray painful experiences, books like *The Bear's Toothache*, by David McPhail, may also help children air feelings and fears regarding pain. Talking about pain with a trusted adult in the nonthreatening atmosphere of a story discussion may, in turn, help reduce the emotional threat of future painful experiences.

Conclusion

Illness and hospitalization present many occurrences that can interfere with the progressive personality development of a young child. By selecting books with a child's needs clearly in mind, and presenting them in an atmosphere in which the child is encouraged to ask questions and express feelings, some of the disturbing aspects of an illness or hospital experience may be considerably reduced. Used in this manner, books can help children understand some important truths:

That parents have not abandoned them in the hospital;

That illness and hospitalization are not meant as punishment;

That there are realistic explanations for bewildering hospital procedures and techniques;

That feelings and fears need not be hidden or denied; and

That adults who understand and care about children will try to help them deal with the emotional stress and strain of hospitalization and illness.

At the same time, open and honest communication, encouraged by books and book discussions, can help interested, concerned adults gain a deeper, more realistic understanding of children's reactions to illness and hospitalization. They may then be able to play an even more effective role in the ongoing, repetitive process of helping children achieve psychological mastery, as well as physical recovery, when illness or hospitalization occurs.

References

BERGMAN, T., and FREUD, A. *Children in the hospital.* New York: International Universities Press, 1966.

BOWLBY, J. Childhood mourning and its implication for psychiatry. *American Journal of Psychiatry,* 1961, *118,* 481–98.

FREUD, A. The role of bodily illness in the mental life of children. *The Psychoanalytic Study of the Child,* 1952, *7,* 69–81.

GEIST, H. *A child goes to the hospital: The psychological aspects of a child going to the hospital.* Springfield, Ill.: Charles C. Thomas, 1965.

HALLER, J. A., TALBERT, J. L., and DOMBRO, R. H. (Eds.). *The hospitalized child and his family.* Baltimore: Johns Hopkins Press, 1967.

KLIMAN, G. Illness in the family. In G. Kliman, *Psychological emergencies of childhood*. New York: Grune & Stratton, 1968.

LESSER, S. O. *Fiction and the unconscious*. New York: Random House, 1957.

OREMLAND, E. K., and OREMLAND, J. D. *The effects of hospitalization on children*. Springfield, Ill.: Charles C. Thomas, 1973.

PETRILLO, M., and SANGER, S. *Emotional care of hospitalized children: An environmental approach*. Philadelphia: J. B. Lippincott, 1972.

PLANK, E. *Working with children in hospitals* (Rev. 2nd ed.). Cleveland: The Press of Case Western Reserve University, 1971.

PRUGH, D. G., STRAUB, E., SANDS, H. H., KIRSCHBAUM, R. M., and LENIHAN, E. A. A study of the emotional reactions of children and families to hospitalization and illness. *American Journal of Orthopsychiatry*, 1953, *23*, 70–106.

ROBERTSON, J. Some responses of young children to loss of maternal care. *Nursing Times*, 1953, *49*, 382–86.

ROBERTSON, J. *Young children in hospitals*. London: Tavisstock Publications, 1958, 1970.

SHORE, M. (Ed.). *Red is the color of hurting: Planning for children in the hospital*. Bethesda, Md.: National Institute of Mental Health, 1965.

SPITZ, R. A. Hospitalism: An inquiry into the genesis of psychiatric conditions in early childhood. *The Psychoanalytic Study of the Child*, 1945, *1*, 53–74.

SPITZ, R. A. Hospitalism: A follow-up report. *The Psychoanalytic Study of the Child*, 1946, *2*, 113–17.

WOLFF, SULA. *Children under stress*. Middlesex, England: Penguin Books, 1969.

Juvenile Bibliography: Books To Help Children Cope with Hospitalization and Illness

Imaginative Stories That Portray Hospital Experiences

BEMELMANS, LUDWIG. *Madeline*. New York: The Viking Press, 1939.

REY, MARGRET, and REY, H. A. *Curious George Goes to the Hospital*. Boston: Houghton Mifflin, 1966.

TAMBURINE, JEAN. *I Think I Will Go to the Hospital*. Nashville, Tenn.: Abingdon Press, 1965.

WEBER, ALFONS. *Elizabeth Gets Well.* Illus. by Jacqueline Blass. New York: Thomas Y. Crowell, 1970.

Information-Type Books About Hospitalization

CHILDREN'S HOSPITAL OF PHILADELPHIA. *Michael's Heart Test.* Philadelphia: The Children's Hospital of Philadelphia, 1967.

CHILDREN'S HOSPITAL OF PHILADELPHIA. *Margaret's Heart Operation.* Philadelphia: The Children's Hospital of Philadelphia, 1969.

CLARK, BETTINA. *Pop-Up Going to the Hospital.* Illus. by Walter Swartz. New York: Random House (undated).

ALTHEA. *Going into Hospital.* Illus. by Maureen Galvani. Cambridge, England: Dinosaur Publications, 1974.

RITCHIE, MARLENE. A Letter to Blackie. In Emma N. Plank, *Working with Children in Hospitals* (Rev. 2nd ed.). Cleveland: The Press of Case Western Reserve University, 1971.

SHAY, ARTHUR. *What Happens When You Go to the Hospital.* Chicago: Reilly & Lee, 1969.

SOBOL, HARRIET LANGSAM. *Jeff's Hospital Book.* Photographs by Patricia Agre. New York: H. Z. Walck, 1975.

STEIN, SARA BONNETT. *A Hospital Story.* Photographs by Doris Phinney. New York: Walker, 1974.

Books Portraying Experiences and Emotions That May Have Special Meaning for the Hospitalized Child

Separation Feelings and the Hospitalized Child

BARCLAY, GAIL. *The Little Brown Gazelle.* Illus. by Kiyo Komoda. New York: Dial Press, 1968.

BROWN, MARGARET WISE. *The Runaway Bunny.* Illus. by Clement Hurd. New York: Harper & Row, 1942.

BROWN, MYRA B. *First Night Away from Home.* Illus. by Dorothy Marino. New York: Franklin Watts, 1960.

KRAUSS, RUTH. *The Bundle Book.* Illus. by Helen Stone. New York: Harper & Row, 1951.

STEINER, CHARLOTTE. *I'd Rather Stay with You.* New York: Seabury Press, 1965.

WABER, BERNARD. *Ira Sleeps Over.* Boston: Houghton Mifflin, 1972.

Nighttime in the Hospital

BORTEN, HELEN. *Do You Hear What I Hear?* New York: Abelard-Schuman, 1960.

BROWN, MARGARET WISE. *Goodnight Moon*. Illus. by Clement Hurd. New York: Harper & Row, 1947.

BROWN, MARGARET WISE. *The Indoor Noisy Book*. Illus. by Leonard Weisgard. New York: Harper & Row, 1942.

BROWN, MARGARET WISE. *The Quiet Noisy Book*. Illus. by Leonard Weisgard. New York: Harper & Row, 1950.

BROWN, MARGARET WISE. *The Summer Noisy Book*. Illus. by Leonard Weisgard. New York: Harper & Row, 1951.

BROWN, MARGARET WISE. *The Winter Noisy Book*. Illus by Charles G. Shaw. New York: Harper & Row, 1947.

HOBAN, RUSSELL. *Bedtime for Frances*. Illus. by Garth Williams. New York: Harper & Row, 1960.

KRAUS, ROBERT. *Goodnight Richard Rabbit*. Illus. by N. M. Bodecker. New York: Springfellow Books and E. P. Dutton & Co., 1972.

LUND, DORIS H. *Did You Ever Dream?* Illus. by Franklin Luke. New York: Parents' Magazine Press, 1969.

MCGOVERN, ANN. *Too Much Noise*. Illus. by Simms Taback. Boston: Houghton Mifflin, 1967.

MEMLING, CARL. *What's in the Dark?* Illus. by John E. Johnson. New York: Parents' Magazine Press, 1971.

SCHNEIDER, NINA. *While Susie Sleeps*. Illus. by Dagmar Wilson. Reading, Mass.: Addison-Wesley Co., 1948.

WERSBA, BARBARA. *Amanda Dreaming*. Illus. by Mercer Mayer. New York: Atheneum, 1973.

ZOLOTOW, CHARLOTTE. *Sleepy Book*. Illus. by Vladimir Bobri. New York: Lothrop, Lee & Shepard Co., 1958.

Self-Esteem and the Hospitalized Child

BISHOP, CLAIRE, and WIESE, KURT. *The Five Chinese Brothers*. New York: Coward-McCann, 1938.

DENNIS, WESLEY. *Flip*. New York: Viking Press, 1941.

FASSLER, JOAN. *One Little Girl*. Illus. by M. Jane Smyth. New York: Behavioral Publications, 1969.

KEATS, EZRA JACK. *Whistle for Willie*. New York: Viking Press, 1964.

KRAUSS, RUTH. *The Carrot Seed*. Illus. by Crockett Johnson. New York: Harper & Row, 1945.

SWIFT, HILDEGARDE H., and WARD, LYND. *The Little Red Lighthouse and the Great Gray Bridge*. New York: Harcourt, Brace & World, 1942.

YASHIMA, TARO. *Crow Boy*. New York: Viking Press, 1955.

Maintaining a Sense of Independence and Autonomy

FLACK, MARJORIE, and WIESE, KURT. *The Story about Ping*. New York: Viking Press, 1933.

MINARIK, ELSE HOLMELUND. *Little Bear*. Illus. by Maurice Sendak. New York: Harper & Brothers, 1957.

POTTER, BEATRIX. *The Tale of Peter Rabbit*. New York: Frederick Warne, 1902.

ZION, GENE. *No Roses for Harry*. Illus. by Margaret Bloy Graham. New York: Harper & Row, 1958.

Encouraging an Open, Honest Expression of Feelings

BLAINE, MARGE. *The Terrible Thing That Happened at Our House*. Illus. by John C. Wallner. New York: Parents' Magazine Press, 1975.

FASSLER, JOAN. *The Boy with a Problem*. Illus. by Stuart Kranz. New York: Behavioral Publications, 1971.

NESS, EVALINE. *Pavo and the Princess*. New York: Charles Scribner's Sons, 1964.

YASHIMA, TARO. *Youngest One*. New York: Viking Press, 1962.

Loneliness

KANTROWITZ, MILDRED. *Maxie*. Illus. by Emily A. McCully. New York: Parents' Magazine Press, 1970.

PERRINE, MARY. *Nannabah's Friend*. Illus. by Leonard Weisgard. Boston: Houghton Mifflin, 1970.

WRIGHT, DARE. *The Lonely Doll*. Garden City, N.Y.: Doubleday, 1957.

Anger

PRESTON, EDNA MITCHELL. *The Temper Tantrum Book*. Illus. by Rainey Bennett. New York: Viking Press, 1969.

SENDAK, MAURICE. *Where the Wild Things Are*. New York: Harper & Row, 1963.

SIMON, NORMA. *I Was So Mad!* Illus. by Dora Leder. Chicago: Albert Whitman, 1974.

VIORST, JUDITH. *Alexander and the Terrible, Horrible, No Good, Very Bad Day*. Illus. by Ray Cruz. New York: Atheneum, 1975.

Fear

CLYMER, ELEANOR. *Chipmunk in the Forest.* Illus. by Ingrid Fetz. New York: Atheneum, 1965.

DALGLIESH, ALICE. *The Bears on Hemlock Mountain.* Illus. by Helen Sewell. New York: Charles Scribner's Sons, 1952.

KRASILOVSKY, PHYLLIS. *Scaredy Cat.* Illus. by Ninon. New York: Macmillan, 1959.

Books To Help Build Personal Courage

ANDERSON, C. W. *Crooked Colt.* New York: Macmillan, 1954.

HUTCHINS, PAT. *Changes, Changes.* New York: Macmillan, 1971.

REYHER, BECKY. *My Mother Is the Most Beautiful Woman in the World.* Illus. by Ruth Gannett. New York: Lothrop, Lee & Shepard, 1945.

Books Describing a Visit to a Doctor's or Dentist's Office

COBB, VICKI. *How the Doctor Knows You're Fine.* Illus. by Anthony Ravielli. Philadelphia: J. B. Lippincott, 1973.

ROCKWELL, HARLOW. *My Doctor.* New York: Macmillan, 1973.

ROCKWELL, HARLOW. *My Dentist.* New York: Greenwillow Books, 1975.

ROGERS, FRED. *Mister Rogers Talks About . . .* Photographs by Myron Papiz. New York: Platt & Munk, 1974.

WAHL, JAN. *Doctor Rabbit.* Illus. by Peter Parnall. New York: Delacorte Press, 1970.

WATSON, JANE WERNER, SWITZER, ROBERT E., and HIRSCHBERG, J. COTTER. *My Friend the Dentist.* Illus. by Hilde Hoffmann. New York: Golden Press, 1972.

WATSON, JANE WERNER, SWITZER, ROBERT E., and HIRSCHBERG, J. COTTER. *My Friend the Doctor.* Illus. by Hilde Hoffmann. New York: Golden Press, 1972.

WOLDE, GUNILLA. *Tommy Goes to the Doctor.* Boston: Houghton Mifflin, 1972.

Stories About Illness or Pain in General

LEXAU, JOAN M. *Benjie on His Own.* Illus. by Don Bolognese. New York: Dial Press, 1970.

McPHAIL, DAVID. *The Bear's Toothache*. Boston: Little, Brown, 1972.

SEGAL, LORE. *Tell Me a Mitzi*. Illus. by Harriet Pincus. New York: Farrar, Straus and Giroux, 1970.

SHARMAT, MARJORIE WEINMAN. *I Want Mama*. Illus. by Emily Arnold McCully. New York: Harper & Row, 1974.

TOBIAS, TOBI. *A Day Off*. Illus. by Ray Cruz. New York: G. P. Putnam's Sons, 1973.

Lifestyle Changes

THERE ARE MANY EVENTS in children's lives that arouse feelings of anger, fear, loneliness, and guilt—events that may create an erosion of a child's positive feelings of self-worth or a dangerous loss of trust in those who love and care for the child. Some events, like moving to a new home, may create minor emotional upsets; others, like a divorce in the family, may arouse deeper anxieties. Numerous writers have suggested ways of helping children cope with situations of this type (Anthony and Koupernik, 1974; Kliman, 1968; Lewis, 1971; Senn and Solnit, 1968; Wolff, 1969). Most agree that how a child deals emotionally with potentially anxiety-provoking situations, will effect his or her future development.

In attempting to cope with such events, and with the feelings they evoke, children can benefit greatly from a relationship with a supportive, understanding adult. The juvenile books discussed in this chapter are suggested for use in such a relationship, as a means of enhancing communication between children and adults. Often, these materials can serve as useful catalysts for discussion, helping to focus attention on issues of crucial importance to young children and their families when situations involving unusual stress arise. Their use can also be illustrative of Janis's concept of emotional inoculation (Janis, 1958), as they present excellent opportunities to introduce children to potentially threatening experiences in small, manageable, harmless amounts, thus strengthening their ability to cope with, and master, stressful situations that may arise in the future.

The materials discussed here are intended to help children face situations that are producing, or could produce, different kinds of emotional stress. They are offered along with the belief that sometimes, out of difficult situations, growth can come.

The New Baby

In the 1940s Martha Wolfenstein wanted to investigate the reactions of mothers and young children to a children's story. For this study (Wolfenstein, 1947) the researcher wanted to use a story that dealt with the birth of a second child in the family. Specifically, she wanted the story to center around a child who expressed some amount of resentment toward the mother and toward the expected or newborn baby. Wolfenstein intended to study the feelings a story of this nature would elicit from pregnant mothers and their preschool-aged children. She also planned to study how each mother's reaction to the story material (e.g., censorious, disapproving, accepting, etc.) would affect her child's response to the same material.

Before proceeding with her study, Wolfenstein had to find an author and artist willing to create a story on the desired theme since few, if any, picture books in the 1940s offered an honest portrayal of a preschooler's reaction to the birth of a sibling.[1] Today, on the contrary, a researcher would find a wide choice of picture books that deal openly and honestly with this subject. Reactions to the arrival of a new baby, including jealousy, resentment, ambivalence, and pride, are frequently portrayed in contemporary picture books. In fact, juvenile books now acknowledge many of the same feelings child development experts have been reporting for some time as characteristic of a preschooler's reaction to the birth of a sibling (Freud, 1935, 1960; Homan, 1970; Jersild, 1968; Stone and Church, 1968).

Individuals who wish to help children adjust to a sibling's birth should familiarize themselves with a sampling of the available juvenile books on this topic, for such books can serve a wide variety of purposes. They can help a child express some honest feelings regarding

[1] The story created for purposes of this study, *Sally, and the Baby and the Rampatan* by Leo Rosten, showed, among other reactions, a child's ambivalence regarding an expected new baby. Results of Wolfenstein's study supported the view that a mother who reads a book to a young child becomes an important transmitting medium of the story material and in this role can have a significant effect upon the child's perception of the story. The study also revealed some interesting aspects of mother–child relationships particularly as to the child's fantasy life.

a new baby's arrival; help adults gain a better understanding of a child's view of this event; further sensitize adults to a child's heightened need for love, reassurance and attention at this time; and sometimes bring to light serious misconceptions a child may harbor about the birth of a sibling.

Thoughtful, caring adults can use such stories again and again to create warm, sharing experiences with young children, experiences that may help a child, and a family too, adapt to a new baby's arrival in an effective and emotionally sound manner.

Several books on the new-baby theme focus attention on a child's feelings of rejection when a new baby arrives. The older child feels better after being reassured that he, too, is loved and needed. *On Mother's Lap*, by Ann Scott, beautifully illustrates this theme. Michael, an Eskimo boy, enjoys rocking back and forth on his mother's lap. One at a time he brings his toys to this comfortable spot. When the new baby cries Michael quickly announces that there is no room for her. But there is room after all, and soon they all snuggle together under the reindeer blanket. Michael's mother reassures him that there is *always* room on mother's lap—especially room for Michael.

The Knee-Baby, by Mary Jarrell, portrays a similar feeling of parental love and warmth toward an older sibling. Here, an older child is offered some quiet time with his mother, without any interruptions from the new baby or anyone else at all.

Other books portray an older child's unhappiness with a new baby even more explicitly. For example, Kevin's initial disappointment in the small, wrinkled, helpless baby who evokes so much attention from his parents and relatives is realistically portrayed in *She Come Bringing Me That Little Baby Girl*, by Eloise Greenfield. Kevin's family, however, successfully enhances his sense of self-worth and importance, so that eventually he begins to view the new baby in a more positive manner. Once again, parental warmth, love, and reassurance are issues emphasized in a new-baby book.

In some books the older-sibling protagonist must run away, or attempt to do so, in order to focus attention on his or her heightened need for love and reassurance when a new baby arrives. *Peter's Chair*, by Ezra Jack Keats, is a simple, sensitive book of this type. Similar feelings are expressed in *A Baby Sister for Frances*, by Russell Hoban, one of a series of well-loved books about a family of badgers—small, furry animals with very humanlike characteristics. In both books the older sibling returns when he or she feels needed or wanted.

Other juvenile books emphasize the role an older sibling can play in helping to care for a new baby. Assisting in the baby's care offers a sibling an opportunity to identify, if only momentarily, with parents or other caring adults, instead of identifying with a helpless, crying baby. Thus, it can be an emotionally growth-producing experience.

In *Peggy's New Brother,* by Eleanor Schick, an older sibling discovers how to entertain the new baby. In *Omoteji's Baby Brother,* by Mary-Joan Gerson, a Nigerian boy finds a way to contribute something unusual and important to his brother's naming ceremony. *Nicky's Sister,* by Barbara Brenner, and *Hush, Jon!,* by Joan Gill, both show siblings who move, at least temporarily, from feelings of anger and resentment to a desire to take part in the new baby's care.

In real life, too, children's reactions to a new baby are apt to fluctuate. One day a child may feel anger and resentment about a baby's arrival; another day the same child may be sincerely eager (or willing) to help with the baby's care. The books discussed above may help parents recognize and acknowledge such feelings in their own children. These books can be helpful on a practical level, too, encouraging parents and children to consider together various ways in which an older child can take part in the care of a new baby.

In addition to involving siblings in a baby's daily care, several books emphasize the role of older siblings in preparing and planning for a baby in advance of its actual arrival. A sensitive, constructive story on this theme is June Jordan's *New Life: New Room.* In this book, three older siblings and their father decide together how to make room for an expected baby in their already crowded apartment. In addition to an honest portrayal of each person's feelings, the urban setting depicted here is a welcome addition to children's books on the new-baby theme, as the overwhelming majority of picture books on this topic are depicted in suburban settings.

Sometimes a book that reveals a glimpse of an older sibling's fantasy life vis-à-vis a new baby will capture and hold a child's attention more readily than a realistic story dealing with this theme. Such fantasy life is presented in *If I Had My Way,* by Norma Klein. Here a young girl, entrusted with the care of her baby brother, imagines how life would be if children were to run the world. In this lively, appealing fantasy, the girl's own parents become two noisy, demanding children, and she herself decides whether or not a new baby should become part of the family. The small girl reluctantly gives up her make-believe world when her parents return. She does not confuse fantasy with reality. She knows that children do *not,* after all, rule the world.

Several juvenile books on the new-baby theme offer parents specific information about how to help an older sibling adapt to a new baby's arrival. Often such books are not fun stories for young children, being information-oriented rather than story-oriented. They can, however, be extremely useful in sensitizing families to important issues that may underlie a young child's emotional response to a new baby.

For example, *Billy and Our New Baby,* by Helene Arnstein, presents valuable suggestions to help adults help a preschool-aged child cope effectively with a new baby's arrival in his or her family. Some conflicting and painful feelings a child may experience at such a time, as well as positive feelings, are sensitively portrayed in this story and further discussed in a note directed to parents. Topics such as Billy's heightened need for parental affection and attention, his desire to be and act like a baby again, and his growing sense of pride and protectiveness toward the new baby are all explored in this book.

That New Baby, by Sara Bonnett Stein, also includes valuable information for parents. This book presents one text for adults, offering direct, practical advice about how to help a sibling adjust to a new baby's arrival. There is a separate text and story line for children. Both the Arnstein book and the Stein book sensitively and realistically portray emotions and experiences surrounding a baby's birth from a sibling's point of view. Both books can become useful springboards for communication between children and adults, encouraging them to explore together the various fears, feelings, and fantasies a baby's birth, or expected birth, may evoke in their own lives.

Hi, New Baby, by Andry and Kratka, also attempts to impart useful information about new babies. This book points out numerous situations older siblings will have to cope with when a new baby arrives. Though presented in picture book form, it is clearly more information-oriented than story-oriented. *Hi, New Baby* does, indeed, convey facts about babies, but it lacks the kind of spark and imagination needed to hold a child's attention.

One of the more successful information-type books on the new-baby theme is Gunilla Wolde's *Betsy's Baby Brother.* This small publication for preschoolers often succeeds in catching and holding a child's attention. It describes in simple terms what a new baby is like, offering honest statements and cheerful, somewhat humorous illustrations. The book shows Betsy's mother caring for the new baby. It also shows Betsy's reactions and occasional participation in the baby's care. The father is not actually portrayed, although he is expected to ar-

rive shortly. *Betsy's Baby Brother* is matter-of-fact in tone and open-ended enough to encourage children to seek information and express feelings about their own family situations. It is rapidly becoming a favorite among books on the new-baby theme (as judged by nursery school children and teachers).

Like other books discussed here, *Betsy's Baby Brother* has evoked some interesting questions:

> Why did Betsy's mother go out and get a new baby? Wasn't the old baby still good?
> Did Betsy's mother know the baby would cry like that and mess like that?
> Was I ever so little? Did I cry like that? What else did I do?
> Did you love me then? Do you love me now?

Simple information-type books like *Betsy's Baby Brother* can be useful in many ways: as a means of presenting information about new babies; as a vehicle for communication between children and adults; as an initiator of make-believe play about families and babies; and as a model to encourage children to create their own stories about a baby's arrival in the family.

Parents, of course, play an important role in helping a child adjust to the changes brought about by the birth of a sibling. All of the books discussed here convey, or attempt to convey, messages for parents. Information-type books offer advice explicitly; storybooks convey similar suggestions by implication. Much of the advice presented in this manner will occur naturally to parents from their own intuition. Discovering a constructive suggestion or recognizing a private emotion in the pages of a juvenile book can, however, provide valuable support for parents attempting to help a child learn how to cope effectively with the arrival of a new brother or sister.

Suggestions for helping an older sibling adjust to a new baby's presence, gathered from the juvenile books discussed here, include the following:

> Enhancing the older child's feelings of self-worth and accomplishment;
> Reminding an older child what it was like when he or she was a baby (how he was fed, bathed, rocked, etc.);
> Answering questions, often stimulated by a baby's birth, about body image, physical capabilities, sexual curiosity, etc., as openly and honestly as possible;
> Warning a child in advance what a new baby is like; e.g., the

baby is small, helpless, wrinkled; it cannot play games and have
fun; it cannot even recognize its own family;

Recognizing that an older child may become angry, demanding,
and jealous when a new baby arrives—that this, too, is part of
growing up and can be accepted and dealt with in a helpful
rather than vindictive manner;

Recognizing that an older sibling can often help with a new baby's
care and that such participation offers children valuable opportunities to identify with parents and other caring adults;

Protecting the older child's rights and feelings when friends and
relatives joyously praise the new baby; and

Offering an older sibling opportunities and encouragement to act
out feelings in play activities and talk—reminding the child
that he can hurt a puppet or a doll, but he may never hurt a
baby.

The child, of course, is not interested in the didactic aspects of
new-baby books. What the young child responds to most is the opportunity these books may offer for a shared story experience with a
warm, communicative adult, an experience that could have a special
meaning—a personal significance—for children who have recently
encountered, or soon will face, a new sibling's arrival.

Moving to a New Home

A family's move to a new home can provide a strain on a child's
concept of himself and the world.

*A human being cannot abandon a loved person without a deep
psychological wound. There is always mourning, even for a person
who was both loved and hated. So it is also for our environment
and physical surroundings. (Kliman, 1968, p. 107)*

Kliman, among others, has pointed out that whether or not we
have been completely happy in our home setting, we are likely to
have invested a considerable amount of psychological energy in
thoughts and feelings about our surroundings. When we move, such
energy must be reinvested, gradually, as we begin to adjust to a new
environment.

Some researchers have observed that certain developmental stages
are particularly vulnerable to upset in moving. For example, Tooley
(1972) has suggested that five- and six-year-olds who are emotionally

occupied with a transfer of allegiance from home to school may be highly susceptible to distress after a family move.

Other researchers have noted that parents who have recently moved sometimes have less time or emotional energy available for young preschool-aged children because of their own eagerness to become adjusted to the new community. A child, therefore, may suffer from loss of a parent's time and attention more than from the actual move itself (Switzer et al., 1961).

The environment itself is sometimes reminiscent of a "transitional object" for a child under three, much like a well-loved blanket or teddy bear.

> *A child cannot hug or go to sleep touching all of his house or sucking on an edge of the room, yet it can be comforting to him to see it and be in it. When he is away he may feel frustrated love and sadness for the now-distant house. (Kliman, 1968, p. 108)*

Placing items important to the child (e.g., crib, bed, favorite chair) in positions similar to those in the old home is one way parents may be able to help a young child orient himself or herself to new surroundings.

Parents, in fact, can help children adjust to a family move in various ways. They can offer honest explanations for an anticipated move; encourage children to express feelings and ask questions about the new setting; and arrange to spend sufficient time with a child in order to facilitate emotional adjustment to the new home and neighborhood. Most important, they can show tolerance and understanding for expressions of sadness or loss that children may exhibit shortly after a move.

A family move, however, does not *have* to be a stress-producing experience. It is, in fact, possible for preschool and primary-grade children to benefit emotionally from the experience. As they adjust to new surroundings, children may take pride in realizing that they have indeed mastered a difficult situation. In addition, when an entire family works together in an attempt to adapt to a changed environment, the family, itself, may grow stronger in the process.

Sharing a familiar book about moving is one way adults can help children express feelings associated with this event. It is one way to initiate the kind of open, honest communication children require in order to face an imminent or actual change in their lives, like a family move, with added emotional strength.

Three excellent picture books about moving show children coping in various ways with this event. In *The New Boy on the Sidewalk,* by Jean Craig, a young boy whose family has recently moved faces and masters a difficult situation in the new neighborhood. At the same time, he discovers a possible friend. Charlotte Zolotow's *The Three Funny Friends* portrays a small girl who is, at first, unhappy and lonely in her family's new home. Later, when she becomes friendly with the boy next door, she begins to feel better about herself, too. Soon her eating and bedtime behavior improve also, and she no longer needs the companionship of imaginary friends, i.e., the three funny friends referred to in the title. In Miriam Cohen's *Will I Have a Friend?* a young boy named Jim feels somewhat reassured and less threatened about being the new boy at school after discovering one potential friend in his new class. This book also shows warm parental support, portraying a father who empathizes with his son's uncertainties about entering a new school for the first time.

Each of these books portrays the kind of fear and anxiety a child may experience when moving to a new home. Each ends on an optimistic note. The endings, however, are believable, showing children expressing honest feelings and attempting to cope, as best they can, with a new situation.

Activities that take place and feelings experienced on the actual day of moving have also been portrayed in children's books. In *Moving Day*, by Tobi Tobias, as small girl shares both happy and sad thoughts with her teddy bear as she watches and helps on moving day. This book portrays a family sorting things out and packing them up. They say good-bye to old friends and familiar places. A realistic air of moving-day confusion is expressed along with the child's urgent desire to hold on to important, familiar objects.

> *no, don't pack Bear*
> *he stays with me*

Finally, the moving van is loaded. Then, once again, the young girl watches and helps as everything is unloaded at the new home. Here she encounters strange sounds, strange rooms, and a makeshift supper served on paper plates. After a while we see the family beginning to settle in, learning more and more about the new house. Next morning the young girl urges Bear to go and see

> *new street*
> *new places*
> *new faces*

Similarly, *Pip Moves Away*, by Myra Brown, conveys a young boy's feelings and fears on moving-day. Reassuring to preschool-aged children is the simple fact that Pip comes along to the new home.

Small boys are never left behind in the midst of moving-day confusion !

Mister Rogers Talks About . . . also helps children understand what moving day is like. Simple words and photographs show children packing their suitcases and *pretending* to move in advance of an actual family move. Feelings of sadness about leaving friends and familiar places are acknowledged. Readers are reminded, however, that they can write letters and sometimes telephone or go back and visit people and places that must be left behind. Mister Rogers also points out that people are sometimes irritable on moving day, partly because there is so much to do. Soon, he assures his readers, a new house will seem like home again.

Children and adults can use this book as a vehicle for communicating some of their own feelings and possible fears regarding an anticipated or recent move. It can also be used to encourage valuable make-believe play in advance of a family's actual move.

When a family from a small village or town moves into a busy, complex, urban setting, the children involved may encounter special difficulties in adjusting to the new situation. A well-loved, award-winning children's book, *Make Way for Ducklings,* by Robert McCloskey, may encourage children to express the feelings and fears such a move may generate. In this story Mr. and Mrs. Mallard and their eight ducklings must adjust to a new home in the Charles River in Boston. Eventually the ducklings do adjust to city life, and the people in the city adjust to them.

Simple, brief questions have been used successfully to relate events in this story to the experiences of children who have themselves recently moved:

How do you think the ducklings felt in their new surroundings?
How did you feel when you first moved here?
Do you know anyone who has just moved to this neighborhood?
How do you think they feel about living here?

A move from one country to another may generate further difficulties in adjustment. *Santiago,* by Pura Belpré, sensitively conveys the emotions of a Puerto Rican boy who has recently moved to the United States. Unfortunately, the storybook solution presented here appears to suggest that a newcomer to this country must do or produce something fantastic in order to be accepted by his or her new neighbors and peers. A skilled discussion leader could, however, turn attention to other methods Santiago might have used to gain acceptance in his new country.

Feelings experienced when a friend moves away have also been portrayed in juvenile books. *Good-bye Kitchen,* by Mildred Kantrowitz, shows a young girl who sits on her front steps and watches intently as moving men carry out numerous boxes and furnishings from a friend's house. The humorous illustrations and the girl's concurrent baby-sitting job may, however, easily divert attention from emotions surrounding this event. The book, however, can still be useful as a means of introducing, and discussing with a young child, a friend's anticipated or recent move.

Janey, by Charlotte Zolotow, also concerns a friend's move. This is the story of a young girl who reminisces in a highly sentimental manner about the many good times she used to have with a friend who has since moved away. The warm, sensitive feelings and the experiences recalled, however, are more likely to be characteristic of a friendship between preadolescents (children in the eight- to twelve-year age range) than the usual picture book audience. The ability to verbalize such feelings, too, is characteristic of a later developmental stage. Older children, who still find picture books acceptable, may well recognize Janey's nostalgic emotions and understand her prolonged sense of loss after a close friend has moved away.

That New Boy, by Mary Lystad, portrays still another view of moving. This book focuses attention on George's feelings as he watches a family with a young boy move into the house across the street. After overcoming an initial reluctance to meet the newcomer, George discovers that he and the new boy share some important interests (e.g., a pet turtle and raccoon), and one suspects that they may after all become friends.

Miriam Schlein's *My House* looks at moving from another point of view. A beautiful sense of "houseness" is portrayed here. The book conveys various emotions experienced when a family first moves into a new home. The emphasis is on the many events that take place, over a period of time, that eventually make a new house feel like home. *My House* depicts warm family ties, too, as members of the family pull together and help each other adapt to the new environment. A sense of security and belonging in the house itself is sensitively affirmed:

> *When a house is your house*
> *You get to know it*
> *like a friend.*
>
> *You understand things about it*
> *that other people don't.*

My House may be particularly helpful for children whose families relocate frequently. The emphasis on how ongoing family life can eventually (and if necessary, repeatedly) make a house feel like home may offer reassurance and comfort when frequent moves must be faced. The book can also stimulate valuable discussion about the feelings and special needs repeated family moves may generate.

Although *My House* depicts a suburban environment, children from a wide variety of home settings have responded warmly to this book. This may be because, as Chukovsky (1968) has pointed out, preschoolers and primary-grade children tend to concentrate their attention on the action and dialogue of a story, often ignoring descriptions or illustrations of physical structures. Books on a similar theme, showing families adjusting successfully to different home settings, would, however, still be valuable additions to the juvenile book field (e.g., books showing families moving into city apartments, military camps, houseboats, etc.).

A House for Everyone, by Betty Miles, also conveys a warm sense of belonging. Although this book does not show an actual family move, it does offer preschool-aged children the comfortable reassurance that everybody has a home and that the reader, too, will always have a home someplace where he or she belongs.

In contrast to the books discussed above, a number of picture books about moving offer immediate, glorious and unrealistic resolutions to a child's understandable trepidation about facing an unknown situation. One book, for example, shows parents happily serving lunch to ten neighborhood children and twenty neighborhood dogs on the very first day in their new home.[2] Another suggests that the joy of finding a doll left behind in the new apartment rapidly diminishes a child's anxieties and concerns about a family move.[3]

Such books only serve to belittle children's true feelings by presenting unnatural and simplistic resolutions to situations involving emotional stress. Fortunately, more suitable books are available today— books that acknowledge children's rights and feelings—books that respect the emotional effort involved when a family is adapting itself to a new home and new environment. Happily we need not settle for trite materials on this topic. The important point, however, is that thoughtful, caring adults can help children gather the strength needed to cope well with a family move, both before and after an actual

[2] Carroll, R., and Carroll, L. *Salt and pepper.* New York: Walck, 1952.
[3] Thompson, V. L. *Sad day glad day.* New York: Holiday House, 1962.

move takes place. Books, and the discussion they stimulate, can play an important part in this process.

Adoption

Psychological parenting has been described as that combination of physical care, emotional warmth, intimacy, reliable guidance, and socialization which all parents offer to their children if they are capable of doing so. The distinction between biological and psychological parenthood has been clearly delineated by Joseph Goldstein, Anna Freud, and Albert Solnit (1973) in their landmark book on child placement, *Beyond the Best Interests of the Child:*

> *Whether any adult becomes the psychological parent of a child is based thus on day-to-day interaction, companionship, and shared experiences. The role can be fulfilled either by a biological parent or by an adoptive parent or by any other caring adult—but never by an absent, inactive adult, whatever his biological or legal relationship to the child may be.* (p. 19)

Adoption, therefore, is not synonymous with stress. An adopted child receiving good psychological parenting has an excellent chance for healthy development. The adoptive parents, however, do have special needs themselves such as the need to recognize and come to terms with their own feelings about adoption. Adopted children, too, will face special emotional issues in the process of growing up such as the desire, often heightened in adolescence, to learn about, and come to terms with, their own biological origins.

Considerable information has been gathered about adoption in recent years. Guides for parents and resource books proliferate. *The Adoption Adviser* (McNamara, 1975), *New Dimensions in Adoption* (Rondell and Murray, 1974), and *Adoption and After* (Raymond and Dywasuk, 1974) are three publications oriented toward parents. The McNamara book offers straightforward, practical information for parents and potential parents about various aspects of adoption. The Rondell and Murray book presents useful, hard-to-find information about interracial adoption and the adoption of older children, handicapped children, and children with other special needs. The Raymond and Dywasuk book is the most psychologically oriented of the three, emphasizing throughout the need for parents to gain insight into their own feelings regarding adoption.

A cultural and historical survey of adoption is offered in *The*

Politics of Adoption by Mary Benet (1976). This book demonstrates how numerous questions concerning adoption have been answered in different ways throughout history and around the world. In addition, Ms. Benet examines the adoptive situation from the point of view of the natural parents, the adoptive parents, the child, and the adoption agency. An outstanding contribution to this book is the foreword by Robert Jay Lifton, which deals openly with the adopted child's ultimate need to find a "connection with those who have gone before" (Lifton, p. 4). Lifton firmly believes that the desire to seek out one's biological origins is a valuable and necessary part of the adopted child's struggle for self-definition and emotional maturity.

Major research studies have also focused considerable attention on adopted children and their families. Often these studies report conflicting findings. It has, for example, been reported that adopted children may be exposed to extra developmental hazards. Schechter et al. (1964) offer substantial evidence to support this view. The authors of a long-term British national survey of adoptive families, however, report that the adopted children in this sample (compared with a cross-section of their age-mates) were doing better, at age seven, than children who stayed with their unmarried mothers and, in fact, better than the cohort as a whole (Seglow, Pringle, and Wedge, 1972).

Bowlby also offers a statement that could be viewed as cautiously optimistic. "It may be supposed that in skilled hands adoption can give a child nearly as good a chance of a happy home life as that of the child brought up in his own home" (1965, p. 132). In reaching this conclusion, Bowlby gives considerable weight to the parents' ability to accept a child whether or not he can measure up to their hopes and wishes for him.

Bowlby, along with others, firmly believes that it is in the best interests of an adopted baby's mental health for him to be adopted soon after birth, thus permitting the optimum arrangement for continuity of mothering and the development of favorable relationships between parents and children. Similarly, Humphrey (1973) notes that an association between delayed placement for adoption and liability to emotional disorders in later development, particularly adolescence, is frequently cited in literature about adopted children. Kadushin (1970), however, offers interesting evidence indicating that "older children can be placed for adoption with the expectation that placement will work out to the satisfaction of the adoptive parents" (p. 211).

The most suitable time and manner in which to inform children of their adoptive status is also open to conflicting interpretations. The majority of contemporary researchers suggest that parents offer this information at the earliest possible time, and proceed to talk about adoption, over the years, in a matter-of-fact, accepting manner, keeping in mind the child's changing emotional and developmental needs and abilities. Others, however, question the efficacy of this procedure and recommend postponing telling a child about his or her adoptive status until the child has consolidated some of the major tasks of development, e.g., somewhere between six and ten years of age.

Jaffee and Fanshel (1970) maintain that the parents' own comfort in talking about the subject is, perhaps, the most important factor in telling a child about his or her adoption:

> *It may well be, however, that it is not so much what and how much is revealed to the adoptee that is the decisive factor in the importance of revelation upon him as it is the degree of comfort or ease his parents experience with their choice of approach. (p. 312)*

A lack of open, honest communication has, in fact, frequently been cited as a major cause of difficulty between adoptive parents and their children (Wolff, 1969). McWhinnie (1967), for example, postulates that a child may sense his parents' reluctance to discuss his origins and therefore refrain from raising embarrassing questions which, in turn, may lead the parents all too readily to conclude that the child is not really interested in the subject. Verbal stalemates of this sort are not uncommon. Books that stimulate communication— books that encourage families to face personal issues openly and honestly—may, therefore, introduce something of considerable value into the adoptive home.

Helpful juvenile publications about adoption do not offer magical answers. Instead, they raise issues, initiate discussion, and offer opportunities for children to reflect upon their own family experiences with the aid of a nonthreatening storybook situation. They can help children recognize that they are not alone in their adoptive status and that other adopted (and nonadopted children, too) have thoughts and feelings similar to their own. They can help parents feel more comfortable in talking about adoption with young children. A book may also have an effect on community attitudes concerning adoption (e.g., attitudes of teachers, peers, neighbors, etc.) by eliciting a personal response when used outside of adoptive homes. A book that touches community members may, in time, help an adopted child find a greater degree of support and acceptance outside of his or her immediate family setting.

Books *alone* will not make a meaningful impact on the many complex issues surrounding adoption. Books on this topic can, however, serve as an important bridge to communication—i.e., as an additional means of reinforcing the potential for healthy psychological growth in young adopted children. They are worth evaluating, therefore, with a "child's best interests" uppermost in mind.

For a long time *The Chosen Baby,* by Valentina Wasson, was considered a classic children's story in the adoption field. Originally published in 1939, *The Chosen Baby* was revised in 1950. Its popularity may have been due, in part, to the fact that few other books dealing with adoption were available at that time. The book is still used by parents, and occasionally recommended by child placement agencies, as a helpful vehicle for explaining adoption to young children.

The emphasis in *The Chosen Baby* is on the chosen quality of a small adopted girl. The story shows a warm, loving family including grandparents, uncles, aunts and cousins. Interestingly, *The Chosen Baby* omits any information concerning the child's birth. Adopted children, however, need to know that they were born just like everyone else, and not created in some unique, mysterious manner. Information about the child's birth could have been a valuable addition to this book.

The Chosen Baby deals well with its initial explanation of adoption. Other aspects of the story, however, are apt to strain the book's credibility. For example, the addition of a new baby to the family is eagerly anticipated by Peter, the family's adopted son, who happily offers to give up his baby things one at a time for his expected new sister. There is no hint of sibling rivalry or resentment. In fact, anger or unhappiness, even of a momentary nature, are not shown at all in this book. *The Chosen Baby* concludes with the simplistic statement, "And Mr. and Mrs. Brown and Peter and Mary are a very happy family." Clearly, a more realistic, less stereotyped story is needed today.

A more recent publication about adoption is a two-volume set by Florence Rondell and Ruth Michaels, consisting of one book for parents and one for children. The children's volume, *The Family That Grew,* recounts the growth and experiences of an adopted child in a sequential, developmental way. Adoption is explained as distinguishable from biological birth. Experiences of infancy and toddlerhood are portrayed, including the child's mastery of various skills, birthday celebrations, and visits from relatives. Although the tone is positive and happy, the book is not grossly oversentimentalized. It acknowledges, for example, that Mommy is angry sometimes; Daddy is bossy occasionally; and some days aren't fun at all. The overriding point, however, is that these individuals are a family and they always will be. The reassurance that temporary emotional upsets do not break up a family is highly valuable. Also valuable is the fact that this story begins by reminding the child that he was born like all other children, a point that is too often neglected in stories dealing with adoption.

Several shortcomings, however, limit the effectiveness of this book. Although oriented toward preschoolers, the book is somewhat wordy for this age level. In addition, it is written in the second person singular; it tells the child reader about him or herself (for example, you were born, you were adopted, you learned to ride your bike). Thus, the distancing quality of an imaginative story is missing. When facts are presented in this style, without the advantage of an intermediary storybook character, a child's own imagination and quest for information can easily be stifled. A skilled adult, however, might be able to counteract this effect by sharing the book in a warm, communicative, leisurely manner, offering the child ample opportunity to verbalize personal concerns or questions about adoption in general, or about his or her own family situation in particular.

The companion volume, *You and Your Child: A Guide for Adoptive Parents,* presents a helpful discussion of the practical and emotional issues surrounding adoption. The emphasis here is on expressing the idea that the adopted child is, and always was, an acceptable and lovable human being. Advice about answering children's questions regarding adoption is also included. Specific answers are not suggested. Parents are encouraged instead to phrase their own answers according to a child's age, vocabulary, understanding, maturity, and line of questioning.

Much in keeping with the view of psychological parenthood expressed by Freud, Solnit, and Goldstein (1973), this guide suggests that the child adopted as a baby has no tie to the biological parents. "The adoptive parents are truly his only 'real' parents because they are the only ones with whom the child has shared the developing life-experience that helps him grasp what parents are" (Rondell and Michaels, p. 38).

You and Your Child: A Guide for Adoptive Parents could serve more than one purpose. It could help strengthen a parent's ability and proclivity to talk about adoption in a straightforward, constructive manner with a young child. It could also be useful at parent group meetings by stimulating open, honest discussion among adoptive parents about issues of mutual concern.

A more contemporary attempt to explain adoption to young children is offered in Judith Meredith's *And Now We Are a Family*. This book attempts to deal realistically with children's fantasies and questions about adoption. It explores some important issues such as what adoption is, how babies are adopted, why parents adopt, and why some parents make the decision to give their child up for adoption. It is questionable, however, whether this publication can become a useful tool to help children talk freely about their own experiences and emotions. For one thing, the book seems to supply too much information too soon. Although proposed as a read-aloud story for young children, and offered as a helpful way to introduce the topic of adoption, it raises complex issues such as illegitimacy. Surely, a preschooler is not developmentally ready to handle such topics. Secondly, the illustrations and calligraphy raise further questions about the book's efficacy. The style suggests a simplistic story for preschoolers, including crayon-like drawings and child-like lettering. The information, on the contrary, particularly the explanation of out-of-wedlock conception, is highly sophisticated, presenting concepts considerably beyond a young child's understanding. In addition, the layout of the book is likely to distract and confuse young readers—a large amount of text spills over, around, and into the various drawings. Finally, the lack of a storybook character and the use of the second person singular in the beginning of the book may serve to quell a child's natural curiosity instead of stimulating discussion and questions.

The most disturbing aspect of this book, however, is the manner in which the author seems to have taken over the child's fantasy life. Concerning his or her biological parents, the child is told:

> *I bet they still think about you sometimes. I'm sure they hope you are happy, and wish you love.*

Further explanations are then offered as to how one adopted baby's story might have begun, including the possibility that perhaps the child's grandparents were angry because they did not believe that babies should be started outside of marriage. Instead of encouraging honest communication between children and adults, such statements might dissuade children from verbalizing their own questions and concerns. The author has, in effect, preempted the child's questions.

And Now We Are a Family is commendable in its intent—to help prevent a child's hurt or suffering in advance of its occurrence. However, the book does not succeed in this regard. It seems, in fact, to deal more with the needs and concerns of adoptive parents than the needs and concerns of adopted children.

Brief statements by Judith Meredith and Alan Gruber, D.S.W., are included at the end of this book. These short postscripts both offer perceptive and helpful information about adoption. They are worth reading in their own right, even if the book's format does not seem suitable for a particular child's intellectual or developmental level.

Other information-type books that may carry special meaning for the adopted child are those providing factual information about sex and reproduction. Few books of this nature mention the adopted child or consider his or her feelings. One noteworthy exception is *Man and Woman,* by Julian May, suggested for eight- to twelve-year-olds. Included in this sex education book is a brief section explaining the nature of adoption, which emphasizes the fact that parents love an adopted child just as much as they would love a baby they had made themselves.

Sometimes the book that is most successful in helping a child face feelings or talk openly and honestly about adoption is one that does not purport to teach about the subject at all. *Abby,* by Jeannette Caines, is an excellent example. This is a simple picture book story about a young adopted girl. The story centers around Abby, a bouncy heroine (who appears to be about five years old), and her older brother, Kevin. The relationship between the two children includes sibling rivalry (brief, but intense) as well as warmth and understanding. Both positive and negative aspects of family life are touched upon. Clearly, Abby feels loved and wanted. Her relationship with her mother is a close and meaningful one. Particularly valuable here is the matter-of-fact allusion to Abby's adoption, which took place when she was about one year old, and the comfortable sense of belonging that characterizes her present place in the family. The family has created a special baby book for Abby which she seems to treasure. This book consists of pictures and information about events important in Abby's life, including experiences surrounding her adoption. It notes where she came from, how old she was when her family adopted her, and what her big brother said when he first saw her—"Ugh, a girl." It also tells about her first visitors, her first words, and other important events in her life. Abby delights in this memory book. She particularly enjoys hearing her brother retell the story, at her urging, again and again. The idea of visually recreating a child's personal history can be a useful means of placing adoption in perspective, particularly for an older child. Personal history books of this type have in fact been recommended as a way of helping older children adjust to new adoptive homes (Neilson, 1972).

Abby, in her warm and exuberant manner, makes adoption seem a part of life—an event that is easily talked about within a family setting and elsewhere, too, at appropriate times.

For older children, *A Quiet Place,* by Rose Blue, serves a similar purpose. Once again, this is not a book that purports to teach about adoption or foster care. Instead, it tells the story of Matthew, a nine-year-old boy living in a foster home. Matthew has already had multiple foster care placements and has spent some time in an institution for orphans as well. The reader discovers Matthew as he is beginning to form closer relationships with his foster family. The story does not deny the existence of emotional stress in Matthew's life. Instead, it acknowledges the real difficulties inherent in recurring traumas of separation and loss.

Matthew discovers a quiet place in the public library where he likes to think about himself and his world. This secret place is very important and comforting to him. When the library is permanently closed, Matthew is faced once again with feelings of loss and despair. Then, with the help of his understanding family, he manages to master this temporary crisis. In fact, Matthew grows emotionally stronger and more secure as the book progresses. The reader is left with the feeling that this excellent foster home placement will become a permanent home for Matthew.

A child actually coping with foster home placement may relate to this book in a special way. He can take what he needs, wants, or is ready and able to absorb from Matthew's story—he can identify closely with Matthew or not at all. The distancing quality of an imaginative fictional character makes this choice possible. The story, therefore, is much less threatening than it would be were it a straightforward nonfiction account of foster home placement.

Questions raised by a sensitive adult may help a child talk about Matthew's story and, if appropriate, talk about himself or herself as well:

1. How did Matthew feel when the Reardons (his first foster parents) became angry at him? How do you feel when your family becomes upset or angry with you?

2. When Matthew felt that he belonged with the Walter family, how did he express this feeling? Did his "Mama" understand?

3. Sometimes Matthew kept his feelings to himself. Sometimes he shared his feelings with "Mama." Is there someone you can share your feelings with? Do you think he or she understands how you feel?

4. Why did Matthew need a quiet place all for himself? Do you have such a place? Can you tell me about it or is it a secret?

In addition to information-type books about adoption and stories in which the protagonist happens to be an adopted or foster child, some books for preschoolers simply introduce the topic of adoption. Such books do not consider or attempt to deal with the many complex issues surrounding adoption. *I Am Adopted,* by Susan Lapsley, for example, could be a useful primer about adoption. This book can be shared with a young child in an easy, comfortable manner as a means of introducing adoption and allowing the child's own imagination or curiosity to lead the way to further discussion. It explains, in language understandable to a preschooler, what it is to be adopted, concluding with the phrase, "Adoption means belonging." Other simple, straightforward books that talk about adoption but do not overwhelm a young child with details unsuited to his or her age or intellect would be welcome additions to the juvenile book field.

Transcultural adoption has received little attention in children's books. One juvenile book dealing with this topic is Pearl Buck's *Welcome Child,* published in 1963. This book tells the story of Kim, a Korean orphan who comes to the United States to be adopted by an American family. Kim meets her adoptive parents for the first time at the airline terminal. Other than feeling somewhat shy, she does not express any particular emotion about the strange environment that confronts her, the strange food and clothing, etc. The very next morning, Kim starts school. Since she is not willing to stay a full day, her mother brings her home again. Kim is assured that she will like school soon—that it will be easy to get to know the children, "for they all like you" (p. 18). Kim does eventually find friends at school. She also becomes more comfortable with her new parents and her two lively brothers.

Sensitive, moving photographs by Alan Haas add greatly to *Welcome Child.* The photographs, by themselves, might provide a useful springboard for discussion, inspiring children and adults to talk about some important issues surrounding transcultural adoption. The narrative, however, does not fully acknowledge the complexity of the adjustments a girl like Kim would be apt to face in her new home setting. A more open, honest appraisal of experiences and feelings surrounding adoption across national and cultural lines would be a welcome addition to the picturebook field.

Jan de Hartog's *The Children: A Personal Record for the Use of Adoptive Parents* is a book for adults that deals with the adoption of two Korean girls (aged five and three) by the author and his wife. This sensitive book is somewhat of a classic in the adoption field. The author's method of coping with the problem of acculturation could furnish important clues for adoptive parents facing similar adjustment problems. Practical suggestions concerning transcultural adoptions are offered. For example, de Hartog recommends placing mattresses on the floor as one possible sleeping arrangement, until a child from Korea becomes accustomed to more typical American bedtime arrangements. Similarly, he cautions Americans to restrain themselves from offering children, newly arrived in this country, a cornucopia of rich foods, which, he notes, is apt to cause anguish, confusion, and diarrhea. Selected anecdotes from this publication could make a beautiful picture book, too, if presented in language and style suitable for young children. A juvenile book, inspired in this manner, could easily become a more useful catalyst for communication among children and adults than the well-intended but oversentimentalized *Welcome Child*.

One aspect of transcultural adoption concerns the adopted child's eventual confrontation with the experience and the reality of being "different." *Chinese Eyes*, by Marjorie Waybill, is a warm, sensitive picture book that can stimulate honest, potentially helpful communication about this occurrence. In addition to its use with adopted children, *Chinese Eyes* can also become a valuable communicative tool in classroom settings which include adopted (and nonadopted) children from different countries.

Parent organizations occasionally publish booklets that may be of special interest to families who have adopted, or are in the process of adopting, children from other countries. One such booklet, *My Journey Home,* by Jackie Partridge,[4] tells the story of how and why a child from Korea is adopted by an American family. It includes space to

---

[4] Available from OURS, 3148 Humboldt Ave. S., Minneapolis, Minn. Similar booklets concerning Vietnamese and Colombian children adopted by American families are available from the same organization.

add a child's own drawings and photographs, thus encouraging a parent to create a personal history book for the child-reader.

Adoptive parents have expressed mixed reactions to these booklets. The description in *My Journey Home* of the Korean child's early background, trip to the United States, and subsequent experiences in this country has been considered helpful. The suggestion, however, that the biological mother took her child to a special place (an orphanage or adoption agency) because she wanted the child to have enough clothes to wear and food to eat, an opportunity to go to school, and so forth, though likely to be realistic, is of questionable value in helping adopted children adjust to a new home. Such statements might heighten anxiety in young children, adopted or nonadopted. Could they be separated from their present families if better food and clothing and a place to go to school suddenly became available elsewhere?

Several kinds of adoption are not sufficiently portrayed in the children's book field. More books are needed that relate well to the experiences of families adopting handicapped children, older children, and children from different racial backgrounds. The trend in this country shows that such adoptions are continuously increasing, while the availability for adoption of healthy, white infants is rapidly decreasing. Books are needed, therefore, that acknowledge the fact that there are different ways that families come together without placing undo emphasis on the adoption of children still in infancy who exhibit certain expected racial characteristics and/or physical normalcy.

Books about families per se can be helpful in this respect. *All Kinds of Families* by Norma Simon, for example, beautifully illustrates different patterns of family life. Joe Lasker's sensitive illustrations do, indeed, show all kinds of families and help convey the idea that a family is the place where most children are nurtured, emotionally as well as physically. Twice in this book, adoption is mentioned as a way in which children become part of a family.

A coloring book prepared by Joan McNamara and Joanne Opel[5] also deals with families and how they are formed. This book, too, offers an opportunity for young children to become familiar with the fact that families can be made up of individuals of varying racial and cultural backgrounds.

Norma Simon's book and the McNamara–Opel coloring book both communicate the idea that warmth, security, and love are, or optimally should be, an integral part of family life. In addition to their

[5] Available from Adoptalk, Ossining, N.Y.

possible special meaning for adopted children, such books may serve an important purpose by helping nonadopted children recognize that classmates or neighbors who are being raised by psychological rather than biological parents need not be considered strange nor deprived.

Animal allegories may also have a personal meaning for children joining families under somewhat special or atypical circumstances. Children and adults alike can spin their own fantasies around such stories without being restricted by prescribed human traits. *Lonesome Little Colt,* by C. W. Anderson, for example, offers a simple but eloquent adoption-type story. In this story, a colt's mother has died. The colt is left alone and lonely, unlike the other colts on the farm who all snuggle close to their mothers. Then a mare whose foal has died is brought to the farm to adopt the small colt. Black-and-white drawings beautifully convey the colt's early sense of aloneness and despair, followed by a warmth and closeness that brings joy to both "mother" and "child." In addition to its use with adopted children, *Lonesome Little Colt* has been found helpful in introducing the concept of adoption to children from nonadoptive homes.

A family arrangement increasingly accepted today is the one-parent family. *Just Momma and Me,* by Christine Eber, describes an adopted daughter's life with her single mother. The young girl apparently enjoys a rather idyllic life which suddenly becomes complicated by the addition of "Momma's" lover, and eventually the arrival of a new baby in the home as well. This story is commendable for its realism; a simpler one on this theme, however, with less distracting and potentially disturbing elements could become a valuable addition to the picturebook field.

They Came To Stay, by Marjorie Margolies, also focuses attention on the experiences of a single adoptive parent. Though this book was written for adults, parts of it could be adapted for sharing with young children. Ms. Margolies adopted one daughter from Korea and one from Vietnam. Her story, written with a collaborator, Ruth Gruber, is sensitive, perceptive, and emotionally moving. In addition to expressing joy and love, it describes some of the special difficulties and feelings children and parents forming families in this manner may face. In addition to stimulating discussion within adoptive homes, this book could be an excellent means of introducing children from nonadoptive homes to the idea that families formed in other than traditional ways can be characterized by warmth, love, and caring.

Adoption across racial lines (such as the adoption of black children by white families) and the adoption of handicapped children are two topics seldom portrayed in juvenile books.

Adoptive parents have reported that picture books about interracial families and stories about families with handicapped children are frequently helpful to them in dealing with their own family experiences, even when such books do not speak about adoption per se. *Black Is Brown Is Tan*, by Arnold Adoff, the story of an interracial family, and *Howie Helps Himself*, by Joan Fassler, the story of a handicapped child, are two possible choices here. Both books show warm, loving families though neither publication includes or suggests adoption. Such books can help generate discussion about families and how they grow, and may serve as useful points of departure for a consideration of the special needs of adopted children of varying, less typical backgrounds.

Sometimes children become fearful and intimidated when they hear that a court proceeding will take place to formalize their adoption. The fact that a child and his or her family must physically appear in court on a specified date can conjure all kinds of anxieties in a youngster's mind. Adults would be astonished if they knew the fears and misconceptions a child may be harboring about this anticipated event. Television has led children to believe that court appearances are likely to involve adversary proceedings; that there are good people and bad people; and that someone may be incarcerated on the spot, "and never be seen or heard from again."

One juvenile publication, therefore, has a special value because of its clear, simple portrayal of the court proceeding in an adoption matter. *Is That Your Sister?*, by Catherine and Sherry Bunin, includes a realistic description of an entire family's appearance in court for the purpose of formalizing the adoption of the younger sister. Such material could become a valuable aid in preparing a child emotionally for a court visit. It could encourage a child to ask questions about the event or spark a dramatization (playacting) of the court appearance in advance of its occurrence, thus helping to make the procedure more familiar and less intimidating to the child. *Is That Your Sister?* can be helpful to adoptive parents in other ways, too. It describes the process of adoption, with refreshing honesty, from a child's point of view. In addition, it happens to be the story of an adoption across racial lines, thus helping to fill a long-existing gap in the children's book field. *Is That Your Sister?* may help children in the six- to eight-year age range view adoption, including interracial adoption, as one way—a compassionate and human way—families may be formed.

Constructive, useful stories about adoption, or reminiscent of adoption, do exist in the children's book field. Individuals in the helping professions and adults interested in talking about adoption with young children should familiarize themselves with such material. They may discover that a carefully selected book can become a valuable communicative-aid—a means of helping children and adults acknowledge feelings and accumulate insights, and a way of helping them deal openly and honestly with a topic of emotional significance in each of their lives.

Divorce

Children of divorce constitute a steadily growing population in the United States.

> *Almost 70 percent of divorcing couples have minor children, and almost 9 million children (or one in seven) are children of divorce. . . . This does not take into account the number of permanent separations or desertions (the poor man's divorce), which are believed to equal the number of legal divorces. If we combine divorce and desertion, about 18 million children in the United States will have experienced a disruption of the parental relationship during the period of their childhood. (Anthony, 1974, p. 462)*

A certain percentage of divorced parents who enter second marriages, divorce again. Children, therefore, may be exposed to repeated, often painful experiences with separation and loss.

Child development experts frequently view divorce as a traumatic experience in the life of a child. Certain risks have been documented in the literature. Anthony (1974), among others, discusses the possibility that children of divorce may develop psychiatric disturbances during childhood, psychiatric disorders in adult life, and a tendency in the future to turn away from marriage, considering it an unsatisfactory mode of human relationship.

Children from divorced families are, indeed, apt to face a gamut of complex personal emotions. They may, for example, feel personally responsible for the discord in their homes. They may require continuous reassurance that they will be loved and cared for by at least one significant, trusted adult. They may need permission and encouragement to express feelings, fears, and fantasies regarding their family situation. Most of all, they will need an adult who can be sensitive to a child's unspoken message—an adult who is willing and able to help a child recognize and work out feelings of anger, sadness, loss, and fear.

Current psychological and psychiatric literature views divorce as a process of stages, each stage capable of producing a psychological impact upon the child. Despert (1962), for example, speaks of "emotional divorce," a period that precedes legal divorce. It is this predivorce stage, Despert believes, that may be the most destructive time emotionally for a child. Later, the period involving actual divorce proceedings may precipitate new disorders or aggravate existing difficulties, involving, for example, regression, somatic disturbances, or sleep difficulties. Other crisis-type reactions—such as guilt, anger, and withdrawal—may also become evident at this time. Postdivorce stress, it has been suggested, may heighten a child's fear of further abandonment. It may also involve the child in loyalty difficulties with parents, attempts to fill a missing parent's role, and hopeless efforts to reunite the divorced parents.

Each child in a family, of course, has his or her own reality to contend with in the context of divorce. What is perceived and felt by one child may not be perceived and felt by another. In addition, the child's sex, age, and previous experiences with stress also play an important role in his or her response to divorce.

There is, thus, no one reaction to divorce. Also, it is clear that divorce does not automatically produce psychiatric disturbance for children. Often, in fact, a divorce in the family can improve a difficult situation for a child (Despert, 1962). Somewhat encouraging, too, is the fact that parents are now more likely than ever before to recognize a need for help (for their children and themselves) in coping with the emotional stress of divorce. Concurrently, mental health professionals are becoming increasingly sensitive to a child's reactions to divorce. Thus, as divorce becomes a more commonly experienced part of childhood, a large group of professionals, paraprofessionals, and parents are attempting to help children cope effectively with the changes brought about by family separations.

Books for children and adults offer interesting possibilities for assistance in this regard. Several juvenile books concerning divorce, written in a sensitive and thought provoking manner, now exist. Guides to help parents explain divorce to young children are also available (Grollman, 1969). Of course, books by themselves will not make divorce any easier. They can, however, serve some important purposes. They can:

Help sensitize adults to the needs of children when a divorce takes place;

Encourage communication between children and adults about the
feelings a divorce may precipitate;

Help children of divorce recognize that their situation is not
unique—other children, too, often experience anger, guilt, confusion, and so on in response to a family separation;

Help children from intact families gain a more realistic understanding of the meaning of divorce in the lives of their friends
and peers;

Offer opportunities to correct serious misconceptions a child may
harbor concerning divorce, such as the commonly held belief
that a divorce in the family may be the child's fault; and

Help children from divorced families (and intact families too)
learn that there are many different ways families choose to live.

A number of juvenile books have been written specifically to help
children understand divorce and learn how to cope effectively with
the feelings, fears, and fantasies it may generate. One of the first
books to appear for children on this topic was Gardner's *The Boys
and Girls Book About Divorce.*

Dr. Gardner talks about divorce in a no-nonsense, realistic manner. He offers honest, direct comments about love, blame, anger, and
shame. Relations with stepparents and with other children are also
discussed.

Clearly, Gardner's book presents more information than a child
can absorb in one reading. Selected sections, however, can be used by
children and adults as springboards for communication. The book
can also be used by mental health professionals to generate discussion among small groups of children each of whom has experienced a
family separation. In this manner attention can be focused on issues
emotionally important to children of divorce. Opportunities to correct
misconceptions about divorce may also arise, such as the erroneous
belief that a child is responsible for a parent's decision to divorce;
that a child can take the place of a missing parent; that parents can
be manipulated by a child into remarrying each other again.

Throughout the book, Gardner emphasizes two points: first, that
parental divorce does not in any way reflect upon the self-worth of a
child; and second, that the child is not alone in his or her feelings and
reactions concerning divorce. Other children, too, often experience
emotions such as hate, anger, and guilt in response to a family
separation.

Gardner's book has often been characterized as avant-garde. He urges his readers to forget about a father who appears not to love them. "Don't beat a dead horse" (p. 106), he cautions them. Advice of this nature, though intended to help a child face facts realistically, has heightened the book's reputation for unconventionality.

In other respects, however, the book is highly traditional. Gardner speaks entirely from the point of view of children living with mothers (or other relatives) and characterizes fathers mainly as Sunday visitors. Nowhere does he consider the possibility that a father may be granted custody of his children except in a brief reminder to the reader that if the parent he is living with should die, there is likely to be another parent who will be able to make a home for him.

Other shortcomings in the Gardner book also become evident. One is the possibility that the book itself may raise more anxiety than a child can handle effectively at a certain time in his or her life. The child may simply not be ready or able to deal with the material offered. Considerable adult help, accompanied by the opportunity to follow his or her own timetable, may be necessary before a child can come to terms with many of the realistic facts presented here.

Secondly, it is apparent that the book was written with middle- and upper-class children in mind. It is a direct reflection of the reactions of patients treated by the author in his work as a child psychiatrist and psychoanalyst in New York City. Families in the lower socio-economic range often find that Gardner's book does not speak directly and honestly to them and does not touch on many of their concerns and anxieties surrounding family separations. For example, Gardner states that a divorced father who lives nearby and seldom visits a child probably doesn't love that child. Families from different backgrounds, however, cite numerous situations that can and have affected visiting arrangements in their own lives, such as legal complications involving support, lack of money, being in jail, being ill, etc.

A book similar to Gardner's publication, based on experiences with a more representative sample of parents and children—geographically, economically, racially, etc.—might, therefore, be a useful addition to the children's book field.

Talking About Divorce: A Dialogue Between Parent and Child, by Earl A. Grollman, is another information-type book about divorce. This publication includes one section for children and one for parents. Its aim is to guide parents and children toward an honest understanding of the meaning of divorce in their lives and to encourage a genuine communication between them.

Important psychological points are stated here. The child-reader is assured that he is not the cause of his parents' divorce. It is suggested that he might be angry or frightened about his family situation, and he is encouraged to express such feelings. He is also urged to accept his parents' decision to obtain a divorce as a final one. "But no matter what you do, Mommy and Daddy will no longer live together" (p. 46). Finally, he is reassured that even though his parents become divorced, they will still take care of him in the best way they know how.

Grollman's book seems reflective of a situation where parents are warm, caring individuals who truly love their children and are deeply concerned about the effect a divorce may have upon their future development. For such a family, this publication offers a useful springboard for sharing feelings.

For children from less empathetic, loving families, however, the book offers considerably less assistance. Clearly, the reassuring conclusion that "You are our child and we will love you always" (p. 53), accompanied by an illustration of two parents jointly holding a protective umbrella over a small child's head, does not depict the situation many children must face when divorce occurs in their families. An adult may be able to help a child-reader recognize where and how his own family situation is different from the one presented here, so that the ensuing dialogue between child and adult can remain as open and honest as possible.

Useful information about divorce is also offered in picturebook form by Cain and Benedek, respectively a social worker and child psychiatrist. *What Would You Do? A Child's Book About Divorce* raises specific issues and questions concerning divorce and asks the reader to react to each situation. The book then presents, with candor, examples of the behavior and feelings expressed by young children who have faced similar situations. The child-reader may get a helpful message here; i.e. that his or her own response to a family separation is normal, shared, and possibly transient. Like the Grollman book, this book also ends with a picture of cooperating parents, each of whom shows considerable love and warmth toward the child, thus conveying a positive, but somewhat idealized view of divorcing families.

The Gardner, Grollman, and Cain–Benedek books are all factual publications. They present no imaginative storybook characters and no distancing quality. They are, indeed, lessons in divorce—albeit, in many respects, straightforward, honest, and compassionate lessons; they are sincere attempts to present difficult material in a manner suited to a young child's emotional needs and cognitive abilities. Their greatest value may be in the encouragement they offer parent and child to share thoughts and feelings of mutual concern; in their attempt to help adults gain a better understanding of a child's perception of divorce; and in the opportunities they present for returning to a particular section or anecdote, again and again, as often as a child needs or desires to do so.

Imaginative stories, however, stories that present no pedantic facts about divorce, serve an entirely different purpose and fill a different need. These are the books that might initiate an unexpected release of feelings—a shock of recognition—an opportunity to work through a personal conflict while reacting to emotional struggles discovered in literature. Often children will take what they can, what they most need from fiction of this type, and ignore the rest.

Many imaginative stories concerning divorce exist today. Each offers something that could win a child's attention, initiate a personal fantasy, carry a secret significance, and help a child absorb the fact that divorce is now a part of his life, too.

"Once there was a little girl called Janeydear" (Goff, p. 3). Her story is told in Beth Goff's *Where Is Daddy? The Story of a Divorce.* Much honest information about divorce is conveyed here. The reader, however, can assimilate this information according to her own emotional needs and abilities. She can identify with the storybook character or remain comfortably removed from Janeydear's experience. She can absorb what touches her, what gains her attention, and she can count on the distancing quality of a storybook situation to protect her, for the moment, from the rest. As her own family situation changes, she may respond to Janeydear in different ways, at different emotional levels.

Janeydear goes through many of the experiences discussed in the Grollman and Gardner books. At first, she is angry, frightened, and confused in response to her parents' divorce. She feels further abandoned when her mother goes out to work. And her grandmother doesn't help much either. In fact, she chases Janeydear's dog, Funny, out of the house. Eventually the adults in her life help Janeydear understand a little more about what is happening. Then Janeydear begins to feel better about herself and her family.

Janeydear's story is neither perfect nor complete. It is, however, an excellent attempt to bridge the gap between fact and fiction in books for young children.

Other picture books touch on divorce in different ways. *Me Day,* by Joan Lexau, for example, speaks directly to a child's fear of abandonment by a parent. When young Rafer receives a message to go to a certain neighborhood store, he unexpectedly finds his father eagerly awaiting him there. Rafer's joy in seeing his father does not preclude his seeking information in his own direct terms. "Did you undivorce me?" Rafer asks. The realism in this story may help clarify some confusing issues in a child's mind surrounding divorce. For example, it is clearly acknowledged that Rafer's father will not return home again because of any effort, action, or wish on his son's part. It is also clear that the family situation has many difficult ramifications—e.g., poverty, bitterness, and loneliness—but Rafer is coping and surviving, and openly expressing his feelings and concerns along the way, too. Although his parents' divorce does require considerable adjustment on his part, it certainly is not the end of the world for Rafer.

Emily and the Klunky Baby and the Next-Door Dog, also by Joan Lexau, takes place in a different setting and focuses attention on feelings of a different nature. Here a young suburban mother seeks some quiet time away from her children to concentrate on her tax return—a chore her husband used to do. She asks her daughter, Emily, to take her small brother outside to play in the snow so that she can work undisturbed. Emily, feeling rejected, packs her "Klunky" baby brother and the next-door dog cozily on her sled and decides to run away and find her daddy. Since she cannot cross streets, she only gets around the block, soon returning home. Now Emily finds her mother emotionally available and ready to offer the important reassurance that Emily is indeed loved and wanted. Child-readers may identify with Emily and recognize her need for added attention from the parent remaining home shortly after a divorce in the family. This book also lends itself well to role-playing, sometimes helping children gain a more mature perspective of a parent's point of view on issues surrounding divorce.

For somewhat older children, Peggy Mann's *My Dad Lives in a Downtown Hotel* focuses attention on other important aspects of a family separation. At first, Joey is convinced that his parents' imminent divorce must be his own fault. Accordingly, he presents a list of good-behavior promises which he hopes will induce his father to return home. Joey brings this list to his father's office only to discover the futility of his scheme. He does, however, learn two important lessons: that his parents' separation is in no way related to any behavior or misbehavior on his part; and that no matter what he does, he will not be able to bring his parents back together again. Their decision to divorce is a final one.

It is not only storybook children who have difficulty accepting the finality of divorce. In a report of a five-year study of 131 children of divorcing families, Wallerstein and Kelly (1977) note that many children, four years after their families had separated, were still holding fast to fantasies of reconciliation.

In *My Dad Lives in a Downtown Hotel,* Joey gradually adjusts to his family situation. He even notices that his father is much more relaxed than he used to be at home. "The thing is, I am not all tied up in knots inside anymore. What I mean, I can relax with you now. I can—enjoy you" (p. 85), his father explains.

When Joey shares his feelings with his friends, he discovers a surprisingly large number of children at school who live in family situations similar to his own. Joey and his friend Pepe make plans for a Secret Club. To gain admission to this club a child must come from a separated or divorced family. No others will be admitted.

In his family life, Joey finds improvements in his relations with both parents after the divorce. With a sensitive combination of realism and encouragement, *My Dad Lives in a Downtown Hotel* conveys an important truism to children: a divorce in the family can often work out better for a child than a home with unhappy, quarreling parents.

A Private Matter, by Kathryn Ewing, also concerns a child of divorced parents. Here, the setting is a comfortable, suburban community. Nine-year-old Marcy establishes a close relationship with the elderly couple who move next door, often turning to the man, Mr. Endicott, as a substitute father. Establishing substitute relationships can be an important and healthy part of a child's adjustment to a family separation. Unfortunately, by the end of the story the relationship between Marcy and Mr. Endicott is threatened by disruption, and, once again, Marcy must face a loss in her life.

Other juvenile books concerning divorce concentrate almost exclusively on "father's weekly visit." In *Lucky Wilma,* by Wendy Kindred, a small girl spends Saturdays with her father. Usually they visit museums, parks, and art galleries. One Saturday morning they simply walk together, spontaneously sharing fun and feelings in the process. With few words and a joyful collection of woodcuts, the author, Wendy Kindred, conveys the satisfaction Wilma and her father derive from this unplanned Saturday activity.

For somewhat older children, Rose Blue's *A Month of Sundays* portrays a young boy's feelings as he copes with his parents' separation. Like Wilma, in *Lucky Wilma,* Jeffrey questions the carefully planned activities that characterize his father's Sunday visits. "We're always doing something extra special" (p. 55), he complains to his Dad. But one Sunday they simply sit on a bench, eating and talking together. Then they play catch in the park for a while. And Jeffrey decides it was the greatest day ever. The book ends with the reminder that there will be lots and lots of Sundays. Once again, the father visitation–theme is emphasized (and perhaps overemphasized) in a juvenile book concerning divorce.

A Book for Jodan, by Marcia Newfield, concerns the effect of divorce in a young girl's life. Here, nine-year-old Jodan moves to California with her mother, while her father stays in Massachusetts. Jodan desperately misses her father. The book ends with a joyous reunion between father and daughter. At this happy meeting, Jodan's father gives her a special memory book he has created just for her; then he holds her in his arms until she falls fast asleep.

These books are sensitive and constructive: they acknowledge children's feelings and demonstrate that life can indeed go on during and after a family separation. The children portrayed come across as real children struggling with, and often mastering, real problems. One wishes, however, that there would be less emphasis on paternal visitations in juvenile books concerning divorce and more emphasis on the ongoing relationship between a child and the significant adult who has responsibility for his or her daily care.

In addition, children's books have yet to reflect an increasing number of nontraditional custody arrangements. Few, if any, juvenile books, for example, portray a divorce in which the father has custody of the children. In this arrangement, mother might be the eagerly welcomed visitor. Also lacking are picture books about a child of divorced parents whose life does *not* include a visiting parent. The fact that a parent without custody may choose not to visit, or be unable to visit, is seldom acknowledged in books for young children.

Also, parental visits in juvenile books are almost always portrayed as positive events in a child's life. Child development experts like Goldstein, Freud, and Solnit (1973), however, point out that visitations themselves may be a source of discontinuity:

> *Children have difficulty in relating positively to, profiting from, and maintaining the contact with two psychological parents who are not in positive contact with each other. Loyalty conflicts are common*

and normal under such conditions and may have devastating con-
sequences by destroying the child's positive relationships to both
parents. (p. 38)

For a young child, these authors maintain that the security of an ongoing, trusting relationship between a child and the parent he or she is living with should be protected at all costs. Visits from the noncustodial parents, they suggest, should be arranged only when the parent responsible for the child's daily care and upbringing believes such visits would be in the child's best interests.

In the picturebook world, however, such flexibility does not exist. Here, children of divorce engage in enthusiastic visits with the parent no longer living at home—and that parent always seems to be the father.

An interesting exception is "Zachary's Divorce," by Linda Sitea, one of the few stories for young children that acknowledges the possibility that custody arrangements may differ from one divorce to the next. Zachary's story realistically depicts a child's point of view concerning divorce. For Zachary, having a divorce means that you wake up in the morning and your daddy is not there because daddy lives in another house now. Zachary's friend Amy, however, finds her daddy at home every morning when she wakes up, but now her mother lives someplace else. Zachary wonders aloud how grown-ups decide which kind of divorce to give you, "the Mommy kind or the Daddy kind" (p. 127).

Zachary's mother is warm and understanding. She tells Zachary that it is okay to be sad and attempts to reassure him about the future:

This is a very new thing that has happened to us. But really, as
time passes, we'll all get used to the divorce and we'll be less and
less sad. (p. 127)

A child-reader may recognize that Zachary (and perhaps he or she, too) will manage quite well as time passes.

Also helpful when families are coping with divorce are stories that show a single parent and child living together. Several such books presently exist. They do not mention divorce, but they do convey the idea that a child and a warm, caring parent can make a comfortable, effective family. Most of these books show a child or children living with a mother.

Joshua's Day, by Sandra Surowiecki, tells about the experiences of a small boy who lives with his photographer mother. Joshua stays at a day-care center while his mother works. His activities at the center are described in some detail. Joshua's mother comes for him at 5 P.M. Dinner, bedtime rituals, and an honest exchange of feelings are also described. The message conveyed is that Joshua and his mother are doing just fine.

Charlotte Zolotow's *A Father Like That* is also the story of a small boy living alone with his mother. Here, the boy deeply wishes he had a father. His father, however, "went away before he was born." The boy imagines what his father would be like if he did have a father, describing the many wonderful things he and his dad would do together. His mother gently brings him back to reality by saying:

> *I like the kind of father*
> *you're talking about.*
> *And in case he never comes,*
> *just remember*
> *when you grow up,*
> *you can be*
> *a father like that yourself!*

I Won't Go Without a Father, by Muriel Stanek, also portrays a boy from a one-parent home. Steve is reluctant to appear at an important school event without a father. When warm, affectionate relatives and friends recognize his need for a substitute male relationship, Steve begins to feel better about himself and his family situation as well.

Finally, in *Martin's Father,* by Margrit Eichler, a father challenges some long-held stereotypes in the picturebook field by undertaking the daily care and upbringing of his son. Martin and his father are shown eating breakfast, having fun, doing the laundry, preparing lunch and dinner, and engaging in bath and bedtime rituals. And every evening, after he tucks him in bed, Martin's father plays a tune for Martin on his xylophone. Here is one book that could encourage open communication for children and fathers living alone together. It is valuable also because of its simple, matter-of-fact acknowledgment that there are different ways children and parents may choose, or plan, to live—and a home consisting of a child and a father is one such way.

In addition to stories about divorce per se, or books about children being raised in one-parent families, other stories sometimes carry a special meaning for children of divorce as well as their friends and peers. Books that help children express feelings can be particularly valuable during periods of heightened stress. *How Do I Feel?,* by Norma Simon, for example, is an excellent selection to encourage communication and help children understand that feelings are important and can be expressed in words. One incident here, showing Grandma and Grandpa in the midst of a serious argument, provides an important note of reassurance for children from intact homes. Soon Grandma and Grandpa are friends again and everyone feels better. Not all arguments end in divorce!

The Boy with a Problem, by Joan Fassler, is also useful in eliciting children's feelings. Here Johnny is disturbed about something, but the story never reveals the cause of his disturbance. Finally, Johnny begins to feel better after a friend listens, truly listens, to what is on his mind. In addition to emphasizing the value of open, honest communication, *The Boy with a Problem* tends to initiate significant personal responses when children are asked, in an accepting permissive manner, what they think Johnny's problem might have been.

All Kinds of Families by Norma Simon conveys the idea that there are many ways families come together or choose to live. The emphasis here is on the sense of belonging and support a family provides. The book suggests that a family can be a mother, a father, and children who are growing up. Also, a family can be a mother and her children, living, loving, working, and sharing, or a father and his children doing the same things. Thus, *All Kinds of Families* simply and quietly acknowledges the fact that one mode of living involves family separations—a situation that children and adults can cope with and master, if necessary.

A Friend Can Help, by Terry Berger, focuses attention on a young girl's relationship with a close friend. Struggling with family disruption, the girl benefits greatly from the loyalty and genuine acceptance of her friend. Sharing feelings with this friend helps her build and maintain emotional strength and self-esteem during a difficult time.

Open, honest discussion generated by such books can further help children integrate divorce-related changes into their own lives.

Apparently juvenile books depicting divorce are now a part of the ecology of childhood. Individuals interested in child health may, therefore, want to consider the possibilities such books may hold for enhancing communication between children and adults, for ameliorating the emotional damage frequently associated with divorce, and for encouraging or facilitating psychological growth. By sharing storybook reactions with a caring, trusted adult, a child's own capacity for coping may expand—and some potentially anxiety-provoking experiences surrounding divorce may, in time, be dealt with more effectively.

References

ANTHONY, J., and KOUPERNIK, C. (Eds.). *The child in his family: Children at psychiatric risk.* New York: John Wiley & Sons, 1974.

JANIS, I. L. Emotion inoculation: Theory and research on effects of preparatory communications. In W. Muensterberger and S. Axelrod (Eds.), *Psychoanalysis and the Social Sciences.* New York: International Universities Press, 1958.

KLIMAN, G. *Psychological emergencies of childhood.* New York: Grune & Stratton, 1968.

LEWIS, M. *Clinical aspects of child development.* Philadelphia: Lea & Febiger, 1971.

SENN, M., and SOLNIT, A. *Problems in child behavior and development.* Philadelphia: Lea & Febiger, 1968.

WOLFF, S. *Children under stress.* London: Allen Lane, The Penguin Press, 1969.

THE NEW BABY

FREUD, A. *Psychoanalysis for teachers and parents.* Boston: Beacon Press, 1935, 1960.

HOMAN, W. E. *Child sense.* New York: Bantam Books, 1970.

JERSILD, A. *Child psychology* (6th ed.). Englewood Cliffs, N.J.: Prentice-Hall, 1968.

STONE, L. J., and CHURCH, J. *Childhood and adolescence.* New York: Random House, 1968.

WOLFENSTEIN, M. The impact of a children's story on mothers and children. *Monographs of the Society for Research in Child Developments,* 1947, *11* (1).

MOVING

CHUKOVSKY, K. *From two to five.* Berkeley: University of California Press, 1968.

KLIMAN, G. *Psychological emergencies of childhood.* New York: Grune & Stratton, 1968.

SWITZER, R. E., et al. The effect of family moves on children. *Mental Hygiene,* 1961, *45,* 528–36.

TOOLEY, K. The role of geographic mobility in some adjustment problems of children and families. *Journal of Child Psychiatry,* 1972, *9* (2), 366–78.

ADOPTION

BENET, M. *The politics of adoption.* New York: The Free Press, 1976.

BOWLBY, J. *Child care and the growth of love* (2nd ed.). Baltimore, Md.: Penguin Books, 1965.

DE HARTOG, J. *The children: A personal record for the use of adoptive parents.* New York: Atheneum, 1969.

GOLDSTEIN, J., FREUD, A., and SOLNIT, A. J. *Beyond the best interests of the child.* New York: The Free Press, 1973.

HUMPHREY, M. E. The adopted child at school. In V. P. Varma (Ed.), *Stresses in children.* London: University of London Press, 1973.

JAFFEE, B., and FANSHEL, D. *How they fared in adoption: A follow-up study.* New York and London: Columbia University Press, 1970.

KADUSHIN, A. *Adopting older children.* New York and London: Columbia University Press, 1970.

LIFTON, R. On the adoption experience. In M. Benet, *The politics of adoption.* New York: The Free Press, 1976.

MARGOLIES, M., and GRUBER, R. *They came to stay.* New York: Coward, McCann & Geoghegan, 1976.

MCNAMARA, J. *The adoption adviser.* New York: Hawthorn Books, 1975.

MCWHINNIE, A. M. *Adopted children: How they grow up.* London: Routledge and Kegan Paul, 1967.

NEILSON, J. Placing older children in adoptive homes. *Children Today,* 1972, *1* (6), 7–13.

RAYMOND, L., and DYWASUK, C. *Adoption and after.* New York: Harper & Row, 1974.

RONDELL, F. R., and MURRAY, A. *New dimensions in adoption.* New York: Crown Publishers, 1974.

SCHECHTER, M. D., CARLSON, P. V., SIMMONS, J. Q., and WORK, H. H. Emotional problems in the adoptee. *Archives of General Psychiatry,* 1964, *10,* 109–18.

SEGLOW, J., PRINGLE, M. L. K., and WEDGE, P. *Growing up adopted: A long-term national study of adopted children and their families.* Slough, Buckinghamshire: National Foundation for Educational Research in England and Wales, 1972.

WOLFF, S. *Children under stress.* London: Allen Lane, The Penguin Press, 1969.

DIVORCE

ANTHONY, E. J. Children at risk from divorce: A review. In E. J. Anthony and C. Koupernik (Eds.), *The child in his family: Children at psychiatric risk* (vol. 3). New York: John Wiley & Sons, 1974.

DESPERT, J. L. *Children of divorce.* Garden City, N.Y.: Doubleday, 1962.

GOLDSTEIN, J., FREUD, A., and SOLNIT, A. J. *Beyond the best interests of the child.* New York: The Free Press, 1973.

GROLLMAN, E. A. (Ed.). *Explaining divorce to children.* Boston: Beacon Press, 1969.

WALLERSTEIN, J., and KELLY, J. Divorce counseling: A community service for famiiles in the midst of divorce. *American Journal of Orthopsychiatry,* 1977, *47,* 4–22.

Juvenile Bibliography: Books Relating to Selected Lifestyle Changes

The New Baby

Books Emphasizing Reassurance and Love for the Older Child

GREENFIELD, ELOISE. *She Come Bringing Me That Little Baby Girl.* Illus. by John Steptoe. Philadelphia: J. P. Lippincott, 1974.

JARRELL, MARY. *The Knee-Baby.* Illus. by Symeon Shimin. New York: Farrar, Straus & Giroux, 1973.

SCOTT, ANN HERBERT. *On Mother's Lap.* Illus. by Glo Coalson. New York: McGraw-Hill, 1972.

Books About Older Siblings Who Attempt To Run Away—but Return When They Feel Loved and Needed

HOBAN, RUSSELL. *A Baby Sister for Frances.* Illus. by Lillian Hoban. New York: Harper & Row, 1964.

KEATS, EZRA JACK. *Peter's Chair.* New York: Harper & Row, 1967.

Books Showing an Older Sibling's Role in Caring for a New Baby

BRENNER, BARBARA. *Nicky's Sister.* Illus. by John E. Johnson. New York: Alfred A. Knopf, 1966.

GERSON, MARY-JOAN. *Omoteji's Baby Brother.* Illus. by Elzia Moon. New York: Henry Z. Walck, 1974.

GILL, JOAN. *Hush, Jon!* Illus. by Tracy Sugarman. New York: Doubleday, 1968.

JORDAN, JUNE. *New Life: New Room.* Illus. by Ray Cruz. New York: Thomas Y. Crowell, 1975.

SCHICK, ELEANOR. *Peggy's New Brother.* New York: Macmillan, 1970.

Story Revealing a Young Child's Fantasy Life When a New Baby Arrives

KLEIN, NORMA. *If I Had My Way.* Illus. by Ray Cruz. New York: Pantheon Books, 1974.

Information-Type Books Describing What It Is Like To Have a New Baby in the Family

ANDRY, ANDREW C., and KRATKA, SUZANNE E. *Hi, New Baby.* Illus. by Thomas Di Grazia. New York: Simon & Schuster, 1970.

ARNSTEIN, HELENE S. *Billy and Our New Baby.* Illus. by M. Jane Smyth. New York: Behavioral Publications, 1973.

STEIN, SARA BONNETT. *That New Baby.* Photographs by Dick Frank. New York: Walker & Co., 1974.

WOLDE, GUNILLA. *Betsy's Baby Brother.* New York: Random House, 1975

Moving

Books Showing Children Coping With a Recent Family Move

COHEN, MIRIAM. *Will I Have a Friend?* Illus. by Lillian Hoban. New York: Macmillan, 1967.

CRAIG, JEAN. *The New Boy on the Sidewalk.* Illus. by Sheila Greenwald. New York: W. W. Norton, 1967.

ZOLOTOW, CHARLOTTE. *The Three Funny Friends.* Illus. by Mary Chalmers. New York: Harper & Row, 1961.

Books Describing Moving-Day Activities

BROWN, MYRA. *Pip Moves Away.* Illus. by Polly Jackson. San Carlos, California: Golden Gate Junior Books, 1967.

ROGERS, FRED. *Mister Rogers Talks About . . . .* Photographs by Myron Papiz. New York: Platt & Munk, 1974.

TOBIAS, TOBI. *Moving Day.* Illus. by Pène du Bois. New York: Alfred A. Knopf, 1976.

Moving from One Country or Setting to Another

BELPRÉ, PURA. *Santiago*. Illus. by Symeon Shimin. New York: Frederick Warne, 1969.

McCLOSKEY, ROBERT. *Make Way for Ducklings*. New York: Viking Press, 1941, 1969.

When a Friend Moves

KANTROWITZ, MILDRED. *Good-bye Kitchen*. Illus. by Mercer Mayer. New York: Parents' Magazine Press, 1972.

ZOLOTOW, CHARLOTTE. *Janey*. Illus. by Ronald Himler. New York: Harper & Row, 1973.

When a Newcomer Arrives

LYSTAD, MARY. *That New Boy*. Illus. by Emily McCully. New York: Crown Publishers, 1973.

Home as a Symbol of Security, Belonging

MILES, BETTY. *A House for Everyone*. Illus. by Joe Lowrey. New York: Alfred A. Knopf, 1958.

SCHLEIN, MIRIAM. *My House*. Illus. by Joe Lasker. Chicago: Albert Whitman, 1971.

Adoption

Books Intended To Help Adults Explain Adoption to Young Children

MAY, JULIAN. *Man and Woman*. Chicago: Follett, 1969.

MEREDITH, JUDITH C. *And Now We Are a Family*. Illus. by Pamela Osborn. Boston: Beacon Press, 1971.

RONDELL, FLORENCE, and MICHAELS, RUTH. *You and Your Child: A Guide for Adoptive Parents* (Rev. ed.). New York: Crown, 1974.

RONDELL, FLORENCE, and MICHAELS, RUTH. *The Family That Grew* (Rev. ed.). Illus. by Judith Epstein and Tom O'Sullivan. New York: Crown, 1974.

WASSON, VALENTINA P. *The Chosen Baby*. Illus. by Hildegarde Woodward. Philadelphia: J. P. Lippincott, 1939, 1950.

Imaginative Stories in Which the Leading Character Happens To Be an Adopted or Foster Child

BLUE, ROSE. *A Quiet Place*. Illus. by Tom Feelings. New York: Franklin Watts, 1969.

CAINES, JEANNETTE. *Abby.* Illus. by Steven Kellogg. New York: Harper & Row, 1973.

Simple Primer-Type Story

LAPSLEY, SUSAN. *I Am Adopted.* Illus. by Michael Charlton. Scarsdale, New York: Bradbury Press, 1974.

Transcultural Adoptions

BUCK, PEARL S. *Welcome Child.* Photographs by Alan D. Haas. New York: John Day, 1963.

DE HARTOG, JAN. *The Children: A Personal Record for the Use of Adoptive Parents.* New York: Atheneum, 1969. (This is an adult book, but parts of the story could be adapted for use with young children.)

PARTRIDGE, JACKIE. *My Journey Home* (from Korea). Minneapolis, Minn.: OURS, not dated.

WAYBILL, MARJORIE ANN. *Chinese Eyes.* Illus. by Pauline Cutrell. Scottdale, Pa.: Herald Press, 1974.

Books That May Have a Special Meaning in Regard to Less Typical Adoptions

ADOFF, ARNOLD. *Black Is Brown Is Tan.* Illus. by Emily McCully. New York: Harper & Row, 1973. (This is not a story about adoption, but has been considered helpful by families adopting children across racial lines.)

ANDERSON, C. W. *Lonesome Little Colt.* New York: Collier Books, 1961.

BUNIN, CATHERINE, and BUNIN, SHERRY. *Is That Your Sister?* New York: Pantheon Books, 1976.

EBER, CHRISTINE. *Just Momma and Me.* Chapel Hill, N.C.: Lollipop Power, 1975.

FASSLER, JOAN. *Howie Helps Himself.* Illus. by Joe Lasker. Chicago: Albert Whitman, 1975. (This is not a story about adoption, but has been considered helpful by families adopting children with physical disabilities.)

MARGOLIES, MARJORIE, and GRUBER, RUTH. *They Came To Stay.* New York: Coward, McCann & Geoghegan, 1976. (Parts of this adult book about a single-parent adoption could be simplified and shared with young children.)

MCNAMARA, JOAN. *Families: A Coloring Book for Families to Share.* Illus. by Joanne Opel. Ossining, N.Y.: Adoptalk, 1976.

SIMON, NORMA. *All Kinds of Families.* Illus. by Joe Lasker. Chicago: Albert Whitman, 1976.

Divorce

Information-Type Books About Divorce

CAIN, BARBARA, and BENEDEK, ELISSA. *What Would You Do? A Child's Book About Divorce.* Illus. by James Cummins. Indianapolis, Ind.: The Saturday Evening Post Company, 1976.

GARDNER, RICHARD A. *The Boys and Girls Book About Divorce.* Illus. by Alfred Lowenheim. New York: Science House, 1970.

GROLLMAN, EARL A. *Talking About Divorce: A Dialogue Between Parent and Child.* Illus. by Alison Cann. Boston: Beacon Press, 1975.

Imaginative Stories Showing Children Coping with Divorce

GOFF, BETH. *Where Is Daddy? The Story of a Divorce.* Illus. by Susan Perl. Boston: Beacon Press, 1969.

LEXAU, JOAN. *Emily and the Klunky Baby and the Next-Door Dog.* Illus. by Martha Alexander. New York: Dial Press, 1972.

LEXAU, JOAN. *Me Day.* Illus. by Robert Weaver. New York: Dial Press, 1971.

MANN, PEGGY. *My Dad Lives in a Downtown Hotel.* Illus. by Richard Cuffari. Garden City, N.Y.: Doubleday, 1973.

EWING, KATHRYN. *A Private Matter.* Illus. by Joan Sandin. New York: Harcourt Brace Jovanovich, 1975.

Divorce Stories Highlighting Visits with Father

BLUE, ROSE. *A Month of Sundays.* Illus. by Ted Lewin. New York: Franklin Watts, 1972.

KINDRED, WENDY. *Lucky Wilma.* New York: Dial Press, 1973.

NEWFIELD, MARCIA. *A Book for Jodan.* Illus. by Diane de Groat. New York: Atheneum, 1975.

Nontraditional Divorce Story Acknowledging the Possibility of Custody by Either Parent

SITEA, LINDA. "Zachary's Divorce." In Thomas, Marlo, et al. (Eds.), *Free To Be You and Me.* New York: McGraw-Hill, 1974, pp. 124–27.

Stories Showing Child and Single Parent Living Alone and Managing Well Together

EICHLER, MARGRIT. *Martin's Father.* Illus. by Bev Magennis. Chapel Hill, N.C.: Lollipop Power, 1971. (Challenges some long-held stereotypes

in the picture-book field by showing a father and son living alone
together.)

STANEK, MURIEL. *I Won't Go Without a Father*. Illus. by Eleanor Mill.
Chicago: Albert Whitman, 1972.

SUROWIECKI, SANDRA. *Joshua's Day*. Illus. by Patricia Riley Lenthall.
Chapel Hill, N.C.: Lollipop Power, 1972.

ZOLOTOW, CHARLOTTE. *A Father Like That*. Illus. by Ben Shecter. New
York: Harper & Row, 1971.

*Stories About Feelings and Families That May Have Special Meaning
for Children of Divorce and/or Their Friends and Peers*

BERGER, TERRY. *A Friend Can Help*. Illus. by Heinz Kluetmeier. Mil-
waukee: Raintree, 1974.

FASSLER, JOAN. *The Boy with a Problem*. Illus. by Stewart Kranz. New
York: Behavioral Publications, 1971.

SIMON, NORMA. *All Kinds of Families*. Illus. by Joe Lasker. Chicago:
Albert Whitman, 1976.

SIMON, NORMA. *How Do I Feel?* Illus. by Joe Lasker. Chicago: Albert
Whitman, 1970.

Other Potentially
Stress-Producing Situations

ALL CHILDREN DURING the course of growing up encounter minor and, occasionally, more serious stress-producing experiences. In addition to the situations already discussed, there are other kinds of stress that can strain a child's coping abilities (e.g., financial difficulties in the family; parent going out to work; changes in the family constellation; imprisonment of a parent; fire, floods and other catastrophes). Often parents intuitively help children master such experiences, responding to a child's signal of distress by offering additional time, attention, and understanding, all of which are valuable aids in helping children master temporary emotional disturbances. Occasionally, events themselves are so overwhelming, or the behavior displayed by a child in response to a particular occurrence is so fraught with anxiety, that outside help is needed. Gerald Caplan (1964), among others, regards crisis intervention as a major technique for preventing future mental ill-health for all members of families involved in crisis-type situations.

The encouragement of open, honest communication is an important part of any attempt, by parents or professionals, to help children cope effectively with stress-producing situations. Children need ample opportunity to ventilate their feelings and correct their misperceptions regarding disturbing events:

> *It is axiomatic that in any situation of sudden stress, children should be allowed to bring out in talk and in play their true*

thoughts and feelings about the events, even if these are aggressive, sadistic and apparently callous. It is equally axiomatic that when the child reveals his misconceptions about what has happened, these should be listened to respectfully, but that at the same time he should have access to knowledge of the facts as they are. (Wolff, 1969, p. 234)

Books or stories portraying fictional characters facing stressful situations can become valuable tools in keeping these important channels of communication open. When such materials are shared by children and sensitive, caring adults, emotional growth may be enhanced for all concerned.

Financial Stress

One situation that can strain a child's coping mechanisms is a financial crisis in the home. Changes in the family's daily life due to financial difficulties should be explained to a young child according to his or her level of maturity and ability to understand. Books can help initiate such discussion.

John Steptoe's books are often set in urban, frequently poor environments. In *Stevie,* Steptoe portrays a young boy who responds with jealousy when his mother takes another child into their home in order to care for him temporarily while his own mother works. Not until Stevie leaves does Robert recognize that in many ways he enjoyed his company. Families undertaking the care of other children on a regular basis may find *Stevie* a valuable aid in talking about the situation.

Evan's Corner, by Elizabeth Hill, also shows a family living with some degree of poverty. This story may help a child from a similar home environment express a need for a small place that he can call his own. Even in a crowded two-room flat, Evan succeeds in finding and benefiting from such a private corner.

Serious economic deprivation has been portrayed in books such as *Sidewalk Story,* by Sharon Mathis, and *The Family Under the Bridge,* by Natalie Carlson. In *Sidewalk Story,* a young girl discovers that her friend's family, consisting of a mother and six children, is being evicted from a neighboring apartment because of lack of money to pay the rent. In *The Family Under the Bridge* three children and their mother, struggling with financial difficulty, find a place to stay

until their situation changes. A gentle hobo befriends the family in their new surroundings and all benefit from this warm, supportive relationship. The family's economic situation, too, eventually improves.

Both stories convey a sense of warmth and love among family members, despite serious economic hardship, and both include thoughtful, caring friends. Each book ends on an optimistic note.

Friday Night Is Papa Night, by Ruth Sonneborn, portrays a family in which the father, because of financial stress, holds two different jobs. His work keeps him away from home five days a week. Friday night the children eagerly await his return. Pedro, the youngest son, calls Friday night "Papa night." For Pedro, his father's homecoming is the best time of the whole week. The wife's role is highly traditional. She does not go out and earn money during this time of financial difficulty. She does, however, keep the family together. The book also conveys a sense of family love and warmth. The suggestion of economic hardship does not diminish this feeling.

In an article entiled "Unemployment and Family Life," Veil et al. (1970) suggest that the destructive emotional effects of unemployment (and related financial difficulties) can frequently be offset by the resilience of the family as a whole. The family most united in feeling and least likely to imprison the breadwinner within a particular work-style or role is the family they consider most resistant to unemployment disaster. *Friday Night Is Papa Night* seems to depict such a family.

Hiding family difficulties seldom protects youngsters. Often, it makes them feel more anxious as they sense the tensions around them. Books that introduce the topic of financial stress can help families talk about similar difficulties in their own lives. By stimulating an honest exchange of feelings, they may encourage emotional growth for all concerned.

Changes in Parents' Working Arrangements

Changes in parents' working arrangements, by choice or because of economic necessity, can also effect the daily life of a child. Here, too, a book can be a useful tool to initiate frank discussion of the situation.

In Anne-Cath. Vestly's *Hello, Aurora,* a young girl and her father decide to do all the homemaking chores. Together they cook the meals, clean the apartment and take care of the baby while the mother, an attorney, goes into town to work. The book portrays a warm-hearted, loving family coping effectively with the reactions of neighbors who are highly skeptical of their living arrangement.

The Terrible Thing That Happened at Our House, by Marge Blaine, also portrays a working mother. Here the mother's return to work creates numerous problems at home, particularly for the daughter who feels more and more neglected. Finally, the girl explodes: "No one cares anymore in this house. No one listens. No one helps you. No one even passes the milk when you need it!" At last the girl is allowed to voice her feelings about the situation. Now both parents truly listen and, in fact, effect numerous changes in daily living in response to their daughter's expressed needs and emotions. The honest sharing of feelings is clearly depicted here as a valuable and praiseworthy endeavor. Mother continues to work, but now the daughter concludes: "Things aren't so terrible at our house anymore. I guess they're a real mother and father after all."

Children often respond to this book by noting, with surprise: "Aurora got angrier and angrier and she held in all her anger. But nothing bad happened when she showed her family how angry she really was. Things even got better after that." Such comments offer adults an excellent opportunity to reassure children that it is permissible and, in fact, wise to express angry feelings in words whenever possible.

Hello, Aurora and *The Terrible Thing That Happened at Our House* have both been used successfully to stimulate discussion of children's reactions to parent's working arrangements.

Changes in Family Constellation

When a member of the family moves away, a child may experience a different kind of stress. A grandparent's departure may be due to illness or death. Open, honest discussion is important at this time, too. Books focusing attention on children and grandparents can be useful aids in encouraging such discussion: e.g., *Grandpa and Me,* by Patricia Gauch; *I Love Gram,* by Ruth Sonneborn; and *Matt's Grandfather,* by Max Lundgren.

A child who has had a close relationship with a grandparent, or one who has been raised in part by a grandparent, will experience a special kind of loss when the grandparent leaves or dies. Books like *Annie and the Old One,* by Miska Miles, and *My Grandpa Died Today,* by Joan Fassler, are good choices to help children verbalize feelings surrounding such experiences.[1]

A grandparent joining the family setting also requires some adjustment. Here, too, an opportunity for an honest sharing of feelings can help children cope effectively with the new arrangement. For children in the eight- to ten-year age range, *Emma's Dilemma,* by Gen LeRoy, could serve as a useful catalyst for discussion about this situation. Emma must make many adjustments when her grandmother moves into the house.

Kliman (1968), among others, suggests that the arrival or departure of a grandparent can be considered a signal from life that "life is identical with change" (p. 112). Such occurrences present valuable opportunities, he notes, for parents to speak with children about the cycle of life and the fact that children are not the only ones who change. Being exposed to the ongoing "changingness" of life is, in Kliman's view, a valuable immunizing process for young children.

In addition to changes in family living when a grandparent leaves or joins the family home, children may be faced with a sibling's departure from home. This can be a time of growth for all concerned. In *May I Visit?,* Charlotte Zolotow tells about an older sibling who has left home and returns to visit her family. Later, her small sister requests assurance that she will also be a welcomed visitor when she is older and that she will be loved and wanted then, just as she is now.

Children often benefit from an opportunity to talk about shifts in responsibility and other changes that may occur after an older sibling moves away. *May I Visit?* can stimulate such discussion.

Other changes effecting the family constellation have also been depicted in children's books. In *Mushy Eggs,* by Florence Adams, a much loved baby-sitter leaves for a job overseas, creating a sense of loss for the two children who have become emotionally dependent upon her care and affection. In *Stevie,*[2] by John Steptoe, a mother regularly cares for a neighbor's child in her own home while the neighbor works, her own child initially responding to this arrangement with jealousy and resentment. In *Just Momma and Me,* Chris-

---

[1] These books have been discussed in Chapter I.

[2] Changes brought about by the birth of a baby (sibling) are discussed in Chapter IV.

tine Eber portrays a young girl who must adjust to the addition of her mother's boyfriend to her comfortable, one-parent home. *I Want Mama,* by Marjorie Sharmat, also shows a change affecting the family composition. Here a mother temporarily leaves home for hospitalization.

Books like these can be useful communicative tools, either during a particular experience or in anticipation of a planned family change. When used in advance of an expected occurrence, they can help an adult prepare a child emotionally for the experience to be faced (sometimes referred to as mastery-in-advance), much like books about hospitalization or the birth of a baby can be useful in helping to prepare a child for a different kind of event.

When a Parent Goes to Prison

When a parent is sent to prison, children are exposed to a departure that is often "wrenching in its suddenness and stigmatizing for those who are left behind" (Sack, Seidler, and Thomas, 1976). Disruption of their homes, interference in family relationships, separation anxieties, loss of respect in the community, social isolation from their peers, and seriously conflicted attitudes toward their parents are some of the painful sequelae imprisonment of a parent may heap (albeit inadvertently) upon children.

Children's responses to parental imprisonment have not been adequately investigated. Some studies, however, do reveal provocative findings. It has been reported, for example, that confinement of a father in jail is frequently accompanied by a depression in school performance of his children. This has been found to occur not only academically, but in important social and psychological characteristics as well (Friedman and Esselstyn, 1965). It has also been reported that pubertal children, both boys and girls, are particularly susceptible to antisocial behavior following a father's incarceration (Sack, Seidler, and Thomas, 1976). Such studies highlight the need, at the time of parental imprisonment or shortly thereafter, for supportive services to help children cope with the manifold stresses involved.

Families usually engage in some form of deception in explaining parental imprisonment to children. Child development experts, however, recommend that here, just as in explaining illness, death, or divorce, a straightforward account of the essential facts might be the best approach (Kliman, 1968). In a study of children's reactions to a father's imprisonment, Sack (1976) interviewed twenty-two children. The six children whose behavior had been rated as normal during interview sessions all showed some mechanism other than denial to explain their father's incarceration.

Books can help children and families acknowledge feelings and verbalize concerns surrounding parental imprisonment. There is, however, a paucity of children's books relating to this topic. Books portraying separation experiences, discussed in Chapter II, may be helpful here. Stories that acknowledge a parent's absence without giving information as to the nature and cause of such absence may have special meaning for children coping with a parent's imprisonment. Paul Zindel's *I Love My Mother,* for example, tells about a small boy living alone with his mother. Mother and son talk about the absent father:

> *When I tell her I miss my father,*
> *she hugs me*
> *and says*
> *he misses me too.*

This book leads easily to questions such as:

Where do you think the boy's father is?
Does the boy think about his father much?
Do you know where your father (mother) is?
Do you visit him (her) sometimes?

Everett Anderson's Christmas Coming, by Lucille Clifton, also creates an opportunity for discussion about an absent parent since Everett contemplates, at one point, what Christmas preparations would be like if only his father were there.

All Kinds of Families, by Norma Simon, considers the imprisonment of a parent even more directly. This book focuses attention on the diverse ways families live. One illustration shows a man in jail being visited by his family. The text suggests that people in a family help each other and try to take care of each other. Here, family warmth and support are portrayed as positive factors in the rehabilitation of an imprisoned adult (parent).

Psychologists, social workers, and other mental health professionals sometimes form discussion groups of children with similar problems. For children in the eight- to ten-year age range, certain

books have been found helpful in encouraging potentially valuable
discussion about parental imprisonment and the emotions it may
evoke. *Marinka, Katinka, and Me (Susie)*, by Winnifred Madison, is
a good choice here. Katinka, a fourth-grader, tells her two closest
friends that her father is in prison. The relationship among the girls
subsequently suffers some ups and downs. Eventually the three girls
resume their friendship, having shared some important feelings in
the interim.

Turn the Next Corner, by Gudrun Alcock, and *Queenie Peavy*,
by Robert Burch, are two books for older children that focus attention on prison situations. *Turn the Next Corner* tells about Ritchie, a
twelve-year-old boy who faces the painful reality of his father's imprisonment for embezzlement. Ritchie's experiences are not uncommon to children in similar situations. They include financial stress in
the family, a move to smaller living quarters, and attempts to make
new friends. His mother's return to work brings Ritchie added household responsibilities. A visit to his father in jail evokes ambivalent
feelings—anger and resentment, but also warmth and love.

Throughout the story, Ritchie struggles to hide the nature of his
father's absence from his new friends. The "secret" however makes
him feel uncomfortable. He soon forms a close friendship with a boy
confined to a wheelchair:

> *In a way, they shared a bond, one he could never reveal to
> Slugger. Slugger had his physical handicap which stayed with
> him every minute. Ritchie had a handicap also, the burden of his
> father. It was sort of fifty-fifty. (Alcock, p. 124)*

After eleven months in jail Ritchie's father is paroled. Difficulties
of adjustment, however, continue to arise. Ritchie soon discovers that
the effects of a prison term are not automatically eradicated when the
prisoner returns home.

Eventually two neighborhood boys recognize a parole officer visiting Ritchie's house and give away his secret. Ritchie's close friends
question him now, and he is forced to acknowledge his father's prison
experience. Ritchie explains the nature of the crime, and for the first
time answers questions about his father's imprisonment in an honest,
straightforward manner. He can't worry about hiding his father's past
anymore. The book ends as Ritchie, with a sense of relief, invites his
friends to come up and meet his father.

Discussion initiated by *Turn the Next Corner* can help thoughtful,
caring adults assist children in acknowledging and coping with the

meaning of parental imprisonment in their own lives. Even without opportunity for discussion, Alcock's story may help a child recognize emotions similar to his own; place himself, in his imagination, in the midst of the story situation (analogize); and perhaps gain the courage needed to verbalize important feelings at a future date.

Queenie Peavy portrays a thirteen-year-old girl coping with the imprisonment of her father, her mother's long working hours, and severe economic hardship. Eventually, Queenie comes to the painful realization that the father whom she idolized was after all only a ne'er-do-well, selfish, and emotionally unresponsive, even to his own child.

There are, unfortunately, children who must learn to accept and acknowledge a parent's weakness—children who may need help to discard fantasies about an ideal parent—a parent who, in reality, does not exist. For such children *Queenie Peavy* may touch a responsive chord. Others may find different aspects of this story personally significant.

In books portraying the imprisonment of a parent, the absent or imprisoned parent is usually the father. When a mother is sent to prison, the situation often includes additional complex ramifications. Frequently, a mother is the major nurturing adult in a child's life. Thus, a young child whose home is suddenly interrupted by the departure of a mother due to imprisonment may suffer a serious interference in development similar to the potentially detrimental effects of certain early-childhood separation experiences described elsewhere in this book (e.g., divorce, hospitalization, or death). The effects on a young child's emotional progress could be devastating even if the mother is only kept in prison pending trial, a period of time that could in fact extend from six months to one year.

Since a child's sense of time is significantly different from an adult's (Goldstein, Freud, and Solnit, 1973), it would seem mandatory that the necessity for this kind of abrupt separation be re-examined. For one thing, arrangements can be considered to keep young children in prison with their mothers. In a recent law review article, Richard Palmer (1972) points out that a mother's incarceration alone does not display the necessary elements of unfitness as a parent. If it is determined that an imprisoned mother *is* fit to care for her child, and the child is of "tender" years (under three), Palmer suggests that the child be placed with the mother in prison. Since the traditional prison atmosphere is not very conducive to the rearing of a child, he further suggests that mothers and children be placed in quarters separate from the main prison population. Some prisons are, in fact, beginning to experiment with child-care facilities, staffed by prisoners, on prison grounds. Where appropriate, such provisions may serve the child's best interests and also play an important role in the mother's rehabilitation.

Further changes in prison policy, on behalf of children of prisoners, should also be considered. Transportation facilities, for example, can be greatly improved so that continuity in family relationships are possible. Often, prisons are located in remote areas, with public transportation unavailable. Sometimes visits from children are not encouraged or not allowed. If, however, regular visits with an imprisoned parent would be a positive event in a child's life, the family should be helped to achieve this goal as effectively as possible. An appropriate room could be set aside, too, so that parents and children could meet and visit in a more family-like situation.

An opportunity for counseling might also be made available to children of prisoners in order to help reduce the negative impact the experience may have upon a child's development. Since families of prisoners may have become suspicious of society's institutions, an outreach effort might be necessary in order to bring such services to young children.

Finally, courts may consider appointing an advocate for the child of an imprisoned parent, so that the interests of the child can be guarded as closely as possible throughout the experience. This would be similar to advocacy procedures recommended by Goldstein, Freud, and Solnit (1973), who urge that advocates be appointed to represent children, as persons in their own right, in adoption, divorce, foster placement, and similar proceedings. Such advocates should, of course, be sufficiently knowledgeable about children and their development to properly represent a child's interests.

As a further means of helping children cope with the pain and emotional upheaval caused by parental imprisonment, prison officials, in consultation with child development experts, might prepare material for children of prisoners, much like hospitals have prepared books and pamphlets to help children cope with hospitalization. Such material can serve as a source of information about an admittedly difficult topic and also as a means of stimulating communication with young children about parental imprisonment.

Children of prisoners have been referred to as forgotten victims. Perhaps, with the stimulation provided by books and book discussions about parental imprisonment and the preparation of new materials focusing attention on this topic, more adults will remember this group and address sufficient attention to their needs and feelings.

It is clear that children's interests must be seriously reexamined in relation to parental incarceration, for surely the imprisonment of an adult was never intended as a means of irrevocably damaging the development of a child.

Fire, Floods, Storms, and Other Emergency Situations

Reliving a frightening experience through words or play can help a child deal effectively with anxieties that might otherwise be suppressed. When accidents, near accidents, fires, floods, severe storms, or similar events occur, a child can be helped considerably by being offered an opportunity to talk about the experience with an understanding adult. Books can be used to initiate such talk and to encourage potentially helpful play activities.

Changes, Changes, by Pat Hutchins, helped one young child who was being treated for burns talk about fire for the first time since his unfortunate experience with fire occurred. This wordless picture book, showing children engaged in make-believe play, focuses attention on a fire truck hurrying to put out a fire. After a trusted, caring adult presented this book in a number of repeated story situations, the child began to recall and verbalize (for the first time) his own frightening experience with fire. Staff agreed that the process of emotional as well as physical healing was enhanced from that point on.

For somewhat older children, *Firestorm,* by Maurine Gee, has also been helpful in initiating open, honest talk about fire. This book portrays the experiences of two young boys who escape from a canyon fire by following the advice of local firemen.

Experiences with floods, too, have been depicted in children's books. *The Big Rain,* by Françoise, for example, is an appealing story for many children, but often carries special meaning for children who have experienced, or have been threatened by the possibility of, a flood. The book is based on an actual flood in the author's own village. It tells how once it rained and rained in Jeanne-Marie's home town. The river rose higher and higher until it flowed over the land. The water came up to the farm where Jeanne-Marie lived with her family. It came into the kitchen and into the barn. After bringing the animals to a safe spot on a hill, the family went upstairs to a second-floor room and waited for help. But help did not come. Jeanne-Marie was frightened. At last two men in a boat arrived and took them to the village where they had some good, hot soup. Later, the rain stopped and the children of the village helped sweep and clean the flooded area. They helped old people and sick people clean the mud from their houses. They put tables and chairs outside to dry. And soon the sun shone again.

Little Toot on the Mississippi, by Hardie Gramatky, also describes a flood experience. Here a small tugboat struggles with and survives a flood of the Mississippi River. Gramatky's tugboat, a favorite children's book character, is resourceful, but also frightened. He is a good catalyst for the sharing of feelings and facts with young children about floods and similar frightening experiences.

Hurricanes, with all the drama, danger, and destruction they bring, have also been portrayed in juvenile books. In *The Day the Hurricane Happened,* by Lonzo Anderson, two young children who live with their parents in a house near the beach experience a hurricane in all its frightening force. The children help prepare for the storm by tying things down, securing the house, and placing bars across doors and windows. Grandpa tells them what to expect. Then powerful winds and much destruction hit the island. The family survives through a difficult time, though realistically frightened and shaken by the experience. Next morning, the sun comes out in all its blazing wonder. The hurricane is over. Tomorrow the family will start patching things up and rebuilding their house.

The setting for this story is the island of St. John in the Virgin Islands. The book, however, can be a valuable communicative tool in any town recovering from a hurricane. No matter how traumatic an event may be, a child can benefit from talking about it openly and honestly with an understanding, caring adult. *The Day the Hurricane Happened* can help inspire such talk.

Other books describe storms of varying kinds and intensities. *The Storm Book,* by Charlotte Zolotow, tells how a summer storm sweeps over the countryside, the city, and the seashore, realistically depicting the gathering storm, its effects on different geographical areas, and the rainbow that finally appears to "show the storm has passed." This is a reassuring, information-type book that often makes storms seem less scary to young children. Similarly, *Flash, Crash, Rumble, and Roll,* by Franklyn Branley, offers factual explanations for the various sounds of a storm.

One section of *Tell Me, Mister Rogers, About* . . . by Fred Rogers also deals with thunder and lightning. Often, Mr. Rogers explains, it is the suddenness or loudness of these phenomena that frightens children the most. "Loud noises and bright lights don't seem so scary," he assures children, "when your favorite grown-ups are near" (Rogers, p. 57).

Books like these can be used to help children understand the nature and meaning of storms. They can help dispel "fear of the unknown." In addition, when children and adults talk about potentially frightening experiences in a comfortable, nonthreatening atmosphere, many of the fears associated with these experiences begin to dissipate. The books described here are good springboards for such discussion.

Umbrella, by Taro Yashima, a delightful, imaginative story, also involves a rainy day. Momo receives a new umbrella and some bright red rainboots on her third birthday and eagerly waits for rain so she can use her new possessions. At last the rain arrives and Momo walks proudly to school with boots and umbrella—one step ahead of her mother. The rain continues unabated and Momo proudly returns home in the same manner, happily listening to the rain splattering her umbrella and splashing her boots.

Children can playact this story. They can also talk about why Momo was so eager to go out in the rain. This can lead naturally to a discussion of feelings and possible fears surrounding inclement weather conditions. Thus, once again, a shared story experience may help bring previously hidden concerns out into the open so that children and adults can consider them together.

Snowstorms also appear frequently in children's books. *City in the Winter,* by Eleanor Schick, portrays a family temporarily housebound by a blizzard. Together, a small boy and his grandmother watch the city come to a standstill as the snow grows deeper and deeper. Together they observe the hush and the beauty of a snow-filled city.

Mary Jo's Grandmother, by Janice Udry, also involves a heavy snowstorm. Here a young girl copes effectively with an emergency when her grandmother suffers a serious fall in the midst of the storm. Mary Jo manages to find her way through the deep snow to summon help for her ailing grandmother. This story may encourage children to talk about their own experiences, both positive and negative, in coping with inclement weather conditions.

Adults can help children cope with these and other potentially stress-producing situations by engaging frequently in open, honest communication with young children; by offering ample opportunities for children to develop warm relationships with trusted, caring individuals; and by remaining sensitive and responsive to children's needs and feelings. Books can enhance this communication process. They can evoke meaningful responses, give validity to important feelings, reveal serious misconceptions, nourish hope, and build confidence. Books, of course, are never a panacea—they are only one of several communication channels available to help children learn about themselves and gather strength to cope with stress-producing situations that may arise in the world around them. Children will take what they can—what they most need—from a story experience, often ignoring the rest. However, as Simon Lesser (1957) pointed out in his study of adult response to fiction, "whenever a reading experience is successful, intrapsychic harmony is furthered to some extent" (p. 290). Surely this holds true for children as well as adults.

The books discussed here are not intended as a definitive selection. They are intended instead to suggest a philosophy about children and books—a philosophy based upon the belief that books relating to a child's inner needs, combined with story experiences initiated by thoughtful, caring adults, *can* and frequently *do* help children grow.

References

CAPLAN, G. *Principles of preventive psychiatry.* New York: Basic Books, 1964.

FRIEDMAN, S., and ESSELSTYN, T. C. The adjustment of children of jail inmates. *Federal Probation,* 1965, *29* (4), 55–59.

GOLDSTEIN, J., FREUD, A., and SOLNIT, A. J. *Beyond the best interests of the child.* New York: The Free Press, 1973.

KLIMAN, G. *Psychological emergencies of childhood.* New York: Grune & Stratton, 1968.

LESSER, S. O. *Fiction and the unconscious.* New York: Random House, 1957.

PALMER, R. The prisoner-mother and her child. *Capital University Law Review,* 1972, *1* (1), 127–44.

SACK, W. H. *The reactions of the children to the imprisonment of a parent.* Paper presented at the meeting of the American Academy of Child Psychiatry, Toronto, Canada, Oct. 1976.

SACK, W. H., SEIDLER, J., and THOMAS, S. The children of imprisoned parents: a psychosocial exploration. *American Journal of Orthopsychiatry,* 1976, *46* (4), 618–27.

VEIL, C., BARAT, C., GIRAULT, M., and SABLIÉRE, M. Unemployment and family life. In E. J. Anthony and C. Koupernik (Eds.), *The child in his family* (vol. 1). New York: John Wiley & Sons, 1970.

WOLFF, S. *Children under stress.* London: Allen Lane, The Penguin Press, 1969.

Juvenile Bibliography: Coping with Other Potentially Stress-Producing Situations

Coping with Poverty (in Varying Degrees)

CARLSON, NATALIE SAVAGE. *The Family Under the Bridge.* Illus. by Garth Williams. New York: Harper & Row, 1958. (Story portraying severe economic hardship.)

HILL, ELIZABETH. *Evan's Corner.* Illus. by Nancy Grossman. New York: Holt, Rinehart & Winston, 1967.

MATHIS, SHARON. *Sidewalk Story.* Illus. by Leo Carty. New York: Viking Press, 1971. (Story portraying severe economic hardship.)

SONNEBORN, RUTH. *Friday Night Is Papa Night.* Illus. by Emily McCully. New York: Viking Press, 1970.

STEPTOE, JOHN. *Stevie.* New York: Harper & Row, 1969.

Changes in Parents' Working Arrangements

BLAINE, MARGE. *The Terrible Thing That Happened at Our House.* Illus. by John C. Wallner. New York: Parents' Magazine, 1975.

VESTLEY, ANNE-CATH. *Hello, Aurora.* Illus. by Leonard Kessler. New York: Thomas Y. Crowell, 1974.

Changes in Family Constellation

Books That May Be Helpful When a Grandparent Leaves the Family Home (i.e., Changes Residence, Dies)

FASSLER, JOAN. *My Grandpa Died Today.* Illus. by Stuart Kranz. New York: Behavioral Publications, 1971.

GAUCH, PATRICIA. *Grandpa and Me.* Illus. by Symeon Shimin. New York: Coward, McCann & Geoghegan, 1972.

LUNDGREN, MAX. *Matt's Grandfather.* Illus. by Fibben Hald. Transl. from the Swedish by Ann Pyk. New York: G. P. Putnam's Sons, 1972.

MILES, MISKA. *Annie and the Old One.* Illus. by Peter Parnall. Boston: Little, Brown, 1971.

SONNEBORN, RUTH. *I Love Gram.* Illus. by Leo Carty. New York: Viking Press, 1971.

When a Grandparent Moves In

LEROY, GEN. *Emma's Dilemma.* New York: Harper & Row, 1975. (Emma must make many adjustments when her grandmother moves into the house.)

Other Changes in Family Composition

ADAMS, FLORENCE. *Mushy Eggs.* Illus. by Marilyn Hirsh. New York: G. P. Putnam's Sons, 1973. (Portrays feelings when a much-loved babysitter leaves for a job overseas.)

EBER, CHRISTINE. *Just Momma and Me.* Chapel Hill, N.C.: Lollipop Power, 1975. (A young girl discovers that her mother's boyfriend will be joining her comfortable, one-parent home.)

SHARMAT, MARJORIE. *I Want Mama.* Illus. by Emily McCully. New York: Harper & Row, 1974. (A mother must leave home for hospitalization.)

STEPTOE, JOHN. *Stevie.* New York: Harper & Row, 1969. (Portrays feelings when a neighbor's child is temporarily added to the family constellation.)

ZOLOTOW, CHARLOTTE. *May I Visit?* Illus. by Erik Blegvad. New York: Harper & Row, 1976. (Portrays younger child's feelings when a sibling leaves home.)

When a Parent Goes to Prison

Stories Portraying Parental Absence That May Have Special Meaning for Children of Prisoners

CLIFTON, LUCILLE. *Everett Anderson's Christmas Coming.* Illus. by Evaline Ness. New York: Holt, Rinehart & Winston, 1971.

ZINDEL, PAUL. *I Love My Mother.* Illus. by John Melo. New York: Harper & Row, 1975.

Picturebook Showing, Among Other Experiences, a Relative (Parent) in Prison

SIMON, NORMA. *All Kinds of Families.* Illus. by Joe Lasker. Chicago: Albert Whitman, 1976.

Books for Older Children in Which a Parent (Father) Goes to Prison

ALCOCK, GUDRUN. *Turn the Next Corner.* New York: Lothrop, Lee & Shepard, 1969.

BURCH, ROBERT. *Queenie Peavy.* Illus. by Jerry Lazare. New York: Viking Press, 1966.

MADISON, WINIFRED. *Marinka, Katinka, and Me (Susie).* Illus. by Miller Pope. Scarsdale, N.Y.: Bradbury Press, 1975.

Fire, Floods, Storms, and Other Emergency Situations

Books Portraying Experiences with Fire

GEE, MAURINE. *Firestorm.* New York: William Morrow, 1968.

HUTCHINS, PAT. *Changes, Changes.* New York: Macmillan, 1971.

Floods, Hurricanes, Lightning, Thunder, and Rain

ANDERSON, LONZO. *The Day the Hurricane Happened.* Illus. by Ann Grifalconi. New York: Charles Scribner's Sons, 1974.

BRANLEY, FRANKLYN. *Flash, Crash, Rumble, and Roll.* Illus. by Ed Emberley. New York: Thomas Y. Crowell, 1964. (Offers explanations for the various sounds of a storm.)

FRANÇOISE. *The Big Rain.* New York: Charles Scribner's Sons, 1961. (Based on an actual flood in the author's own village.)

GRAMATKY, HARDIE. *Little Toot on the Mississippi.* New York: G. P. Putnam's Sons, 1973. (A favorite tugboat survives a flood of the Mississippi River.)

ROGERS, FRED. *Tell Me, Mister Rogers, About . . .* Photographs by Sheldon Secunda. New York: Platt & Munk, 1975. (Mr. Rogers talks about lightning and thunder, among other topics.)

YASHIMA, TARO. *Umbrella.* New York: Viking Press, 1958.

ZOLOTOW, CHARLOTTE. *The Storm Book.* Illus. by Margaret Graham. New York: Harper & Row, 1952.

Blizzards and Snowstorms

SCHICK, ELEANOR. *City in the Winter.* New York: Macmillan, 1970.

UDRY, JANICE MAY. *Mary Jo's Grandmother.* Illus. by Eleanor Mill. Chicago: Albert Whitman, 1972.

Index of Juvenile Book Authors and Titles

This Index lists authors and titles of juvenile books recommended by the author of this present volume. Other juvenile materials appear, along with reference works and topical citations, in the General Index.

Abby (Caines), 107–108
About Dying (Stein), 19–20
Adams, Florence, 140
Adoff, Arnold, 113
Alcock, Gudrun, 144
Alexander and the Terrible, Horrible, No Good, Very Bad Day (Viorst), 71
All Kinds of Families (Simon), 111, 126, 143
Althea, 60
Amanda Dreaming (Wersba), 34, 65
Amos & Boris (Steig), 43
And Now We Are a Family (Meredith), 106–107
Anderson, C. W., 112
Anderson, Clarence, 74
Anderson, Lonzo, 149
Andry, Andrew C., 90
Annie and the Old One (Miles), 11–13, 140
Arnstein, Helene, 90

Baby Sister for Frances, A (Hoban), 88
Barclay, Gail, 63
Be Good Harry (Chalmers), 39
Bear Who Saw the Spring, The (Kuskin), 3
Bears on Hemlock Mountain, The (Dalgliesh), 72
Bear's Toothache, The (McPhail), 78
Beckman, Kaj, 31
Bedtime for Frances (Hoban), 33, 64
Belpré, Pura, 97
Bemelmans, Ludwig, 52
Benedek, Elissa, 118
Benjie on His Own (Lexau), 78
Benjy's Bird (Simon), 44
Benjy's Blanket (Brown), 32
Berger, Terry, 126
Betsy's Baby Brother (Wolde), 90–92
Big Rain, The (Françoise), 148

Billy and Our New Baby (Arnstein), 90
Bishop, Claire, 66
Black Is Brown Is Tan (Adoff), 113
Blaine, Marge, 70, 139
Bleeker, Sonia, 18–19
Blue, Rose, 38, 108, 121
Blueberries for Sal (McCloskey), 42
Book for Jodan, A (Newfield), 122
Borten, Helen, 65
Boy with a Problem, The (Fassler), 68–69, 126
Boys and Girls Book About Divorce, The (Gardner), 116–117
Branley, Franklyn, 149
Breinburg, Petronella, 38
Brenner, Barbara, 89
Brown, Margaret Wise, 3, 29, 31, 64, 65
Brown, Myra B., 32, 40, 63, 96
Buck, Pearl, 109
Buckley, Helen, 9
Bundle Book, The (Krauss), 28, 64
Bunin, Catherine, 113
Bunin, Sherry, 113
Burch, Robert, 144

Cain, Barbara, 118
Caines, Jeannette, 107
Carlson, Natalie, 136
Carrot Seed, The (Krauss), 67
Cathy's First School (Katzoff), 36–38
Chalmers, Mary, 39
Changes, Changes (Hutchins), 74, 148
Charlotte's Web (White), 21
Children's Dream Book, The (Heller), 34
Child's Book of Dreams, A (de Regniers), 34
Chinese Eyes (Waybill), 110
Chipmunk in the Forest (Clymer), 72
Chosen Baby, The (Wasson), 104
City in the Winter (Schick), 151

Clark, Bettina, 59
Clifton, Lucille, 143
Clymer, Eleanor, 72
Cobb, Vicki, 77
Cohen, Miriam, 35, 43, 96
Craig, Jean, 96
Crooked Colt (Anderson), 74
Crow Boy (Yashima), 67
Curious George Goes to the Hospital
  (Rey), 52–55

Dalgliesh, Alice, 72
Day Off, A (Tobias), 78
Day the Hurricane Happened, The
  (Anderson), 149
Dead Bird, The (Brown), 3–5
Dennis, Wesley, 66
de Paola, Tomie, 15
de Regniers, Beatrice Schenk, 34
Did You Ever Dream? (Lund), 34, 65
Do You Hear What I Hear? (Borten),
  65
Dobrin, Arnold, 13
Doctor Rabbit (Wahl), 77
Drink for Little Red Diker, A (Thayer),
  35

Eber, Christine, 112, 142
Eichler, Margrit, 125
Elizabeth Gets Well (Weber), 56–57
*Emily and the Klunky Baby and the
  Next-Door Dog* (Lexau), 120
Emma's Dilemma (LeRoy), 140
Evan's Corner (Hill), 136
Everett Anderson's Christmas Coming
  (Clifton), 143
Ewing, Kathryn, 121

Family That Grew, The (Rondell),
  104–105
Family Under the Bridge, The (Carl-
  son), 136–138
Fassler, Joan, 13, 67, 68, 113, 126, 140
Father Like That, A (Zolotow), 16, 125
Firestorm (Gee), 148
First Night Away from Home (Brown),
  39, 40, 63
Five Chinese Brothers, The (Bishop),
  66
Flack, Marjorie, 67
Flash, Crash, Rumble, and Roll
  (Branley), 149
Flip (Dennis), 66
Fontane, Theodor, 15, 16
Françoise, 148
Friday Night Is Papa Night (Sonne-
  born), 138
Friend Can Help, A (Berger), 126

Gardner, Richard A., 116, 117, 118
Gauch, Patricia, 9, 139
Gee, Maurine, 148
Gerson, Mary-Joan, 89
Gill, Joan, 89
Goff, Beth, 119
Going into Hospital (Althea), 60–61
Good-bye Kitchen (Kantrowitz), 98
Goodnight Moon (Brown), 31, 64
Goodnight Orange Monster (Lifton),
  33
Goodnight Richard Rabbit (Kraus), 32,
  64
Gramatky, Hardie, 149
Grandfather and I (Buckley), 9
Grandmother and I (Buckley), 9
Grandpa and Me (Gauch), 9, 139
Greenfield, Eloise, 88
Grollman, Earl A., 117, 118, 119
Growing Story, The (Krauss), 3
Growing Time (Warburg), 6
Gruber, Alan, 107
Gruber, Ruth, 112

Hang Tough, Paul Mather (Slote), 20–
  21
Heller, Friedrich C., 34
Hello, Aurora (Vestley), 138–139
Hello Henry (Vogel), 40
Hi, New Baby (Andry), 90
Hill, Elizabeth, 136
Hoban, Russell, 33, 64, 88
Hospital Story, A (Stein), 59–60
House for Everyone, A (Miles), 99
How Do I Feel? (Simon), 125–126
How the Doctor Knows You're Fine
  (Cobb), 77
Howie Helps Himself (Fassler), 113
Hush, Jon! (Gill), 89
Hutchins, Pat, 74, 148

I Am Adopted (Lapsley), 109
I Am Here: Yo Estoy Aqui (Blue), 38–
  39
I Have a Horse of My Own (Zolotow),
  34
I Love Gram (Sonneborn), 9, 139
I Love My Mother (Zindel), 143
I Think I Will Go to the Hospital
  (Tamburine), 55–56
I Want Mama (Sharmat), 11, 78, 142
I Was So Mad! (Simon), 71
I Won't Go Without a Father (Stanek),
  16, 17, 125
I'd Rather Stay with You (Steiner),
  34–35, 63
If I Had My Way (Klein), 89
Indoor Noisy Book, The (Brown), 65

Ira Sleeps Over (Waber), 39–40
Is That Your Sister? (Bunin), 113

Janey (Zolotow), 98
Jarrell, Mary, 88
Jeff's Hospital Book (Sobol), 60
Jordan, June, 89
Joshua's Day (Surowiecki), 124–125
Just Momma and Me (Eber), 112, 140–142

Kantrowitz, Mildred, 70, 98
Katzoff, Betty, 36
Keats, Ezra Jack, 66, 88
Kindred, Wendy, 121
Klein, Norma, 89
Knee-Baby, The (Jarrell), 88
Krasilovsky, Phyllis, 72
Kratka, Suzanne E., 90
Kraus, Robert, 32, 64
Krauss, Ruth, 3, 28, 64, 67
Kuskin, Karla, 3

Lamorisse, Albert, 6
Lapsley, Susan, 109
Lasker, Joe, 111
LeRoy, Gen, 140
Letter to Blackie, A (Ritchie), 61
Lexau, Joan, 78, 120
Life and Death (Zim), 18–19
Lifton, Betty Jean, 33
Lisa Cannot Sleep (Beckman), 31–32
Little Bear books (Minarik), 68
Little Bear's Friend (Minarik), 42
Little Brown Gazelle, The (Barclay), 63–64
Little Red Lighthouse and the Great Gray Bridge, The (Swift), 67
Little Toot on the Mississippi (Gramatky), 149
Lonely Doll, The (Wright), 70
Lonesome Little Colt (Anderson), 112
Lucky Wilma (Kindred), 121, 122
Lund, Doris, 34, 65
Lundgren, Max, 9, 139
Lystad, Mary, 98

McCloskey, Robert, 3, 42, 97
McGovern, Ann, 65
McPhail, David, 78
Madeline (Bemelmans), 52–55
Madison, Winnifred, 144
Make Way for Ducklings (McCloskey), 97
Man and Woman (May), 107
Mann, Peggy, 120
Mannheim, Grete, 36
Margaret's Heart Operation (Children's Hospital), 61

Margolies, Marjorie, 112
Marinka, Katinka, and Me (Susie) (Madison), 144
Martin's Father (Eichler), 125
Mary Jo's Grandmother (Udry), 151
Mathis, Sharon, 136
Matt's Grandfather (Lundgen), 9, 139
Maxie (Kantrowitz), 70
May I Visit? (Zolotow), 140
May, Julian, 107
Mayer, Mercer, 33
Me Day (Lexau), 119–120
Memling, Carl, 65
Menninger Clinic Series, 75
Meredith, Judith, 106, 107
Michael's Heart Test (Children's Hospital), 61
Michaels, Ruth, 104, 105
Mike's House (Sauer), 40–42
Miles, Betty, 99
Miles, Miska, 11, 140
Minarik, Else H., 42, 68
Mister Rogers Talks About . . . (Rogers), 75–77, 97
Month of Sundays, A (Blue), 121, 122
Moving Day (Tobias), 96
Mushy Eggs (Adams), 140
My Dad Lives in a Downtown Hotel (Mann), 120–121
My Dentist (Rockwell), 75
My Doctor (Rockwell), 75
My Friend the Dentist (Watson), 75
My Friend the Doctor (Watson), 75
My Grandpa Died Today (Fassler), 13–14, 140
My House (Schlein), 98–99
My Mother Is the Most Beautiful Woman in the World (Reyher), 42, 73

Nana Upstairs and Nana Downstairs (de Paola), 15–16
Nannabah's Friend (Perrine), 70
Ness, Evaline, 16, 69
New Boy on the Sidewalk, The (Craig), 95–96
New Life: New Room (Jordan), 89
New Teacher, The (Cohen), 43
Newfield, Marcia, 122
Nicky's Sister (Brenner), 89
No Roses for Harry (Zion), 67

Omoteji's Baby Brother (Gerson), 89
On Mother's Lap (Scott), 88
One Little Girl (Fassler), 67

Pavo and the Princess (Ness), 69–70
Peggy's New Brother (Schick), 89
Perrine, Mary, 70

Peter's Chair (Keats), 88
Pip Moves Away (Brown), 96
Pop-Up Going to the Hospital
  (Clark), 59
Potter, Beatrix, 67
Preston, Edna, 71
Private Matter, A (Ewing), 121

Queenie Peavy (Burch), 144, 146
Quiet Noisy Book, The (Brown), 65
Quiet Place, A (Blue), 108–109

Red Balloon, The (Lamorisee), 6–7
Rey, H. A., 52
Rey, Margaret, 52
Reyher, Becky, 42, 73
Ritchie, Marlene, 61
Rockwell, Harlow, 75
Rogers, Fred, 75, 97, 151
Rondell, Florence, 104, 105
Rosten, Leo, 87
Runaway Bunny, The (Brown), 29, 64

Sally and the Baby and the Rampatan
  (Rosten), 87
Sam, Bangs & Moonshine (Ness), 16
Santiago (Belpré), 97
Sauer, Julia L., 40
Scaredy Cat (Krasilovsky), 72
Scat (Dobrin), 13
Schick, Eleanor, 89, 151
Schlein, Miriam, 29, 98
Schneider, Nina, 31, 64
Scott, Ann, 88
Segal, Lore, 78
Sendak, Maurice, 71
Sharmat, Marjorie W., 11, 78, 142
Shawn Goes to School (Breinburg), 38
Shay, Arthur, 58
She Come Bringing Me That Little Baby
  Girl (Greenfield), 88
Sidewalk Story (Mathis), 136
Simon, Norma, 44, 71, 111, 126, 143
Sir Ribbeck of Ribbeck of Havelland
  (Fontane), 15
Sitea, Linda, 124
Sleepy Book (Zolotow), 31, 64
Slote, Alfred, 20
Smith, Doris B., 20
Sobol, Harriet, 60
Sonneborn, Ruth, 9, 138, 139
Stanek, Muriel, 16, 125
Steig, William, 43
Stein, Sara Bonnett, 19, 59, 90
Steiner, Charlotte, 34, 63
Steptoe, John, 136, 140
Stevie (Steptoe), 136, 140
Storm Book, The (Zolotow), 149

Story About Ping, The (Flack), 67–68
Summer Noisy Book, The (Brown), 65
Surowiecki, Sandra, 124
Swift, Hildegarde, 67

Tale of Peter Rabbit, The (Potter), 67
Talking About Divorce: A Dialogue Be-
  tween Parent and Child (Grollman),
  117–118
Tamburine, Jean, 55
Taste of Blackberries, A (Smith), 20
Tell Me a Mitzi (Segal), 78
Tell Me, Mister Rogers, About . . .
  (Rogers), 151
Temper Tantrum Book, The (Preston),
  71
Tenth Good Thing About Barney, The
  (Viorst), 5
Terrible Thing That Happened at Our
  House, The (Blaine), 70, 139
That New Baby (Stein), 90
That New Boy (Lystad), 98
Thayer, Jane, 35
There's a Nightmare in My Closet
  (Mayer), 33
They Came to Stay (Margolies), 112
Three Funny Friends, The (Zolotow),
  96
Time of Wonder (McCloskey), 3
Tobias, Tobi, 78, 96
Tommy Goes to the Doctor (Wolde),
  75
Too Much Noise (McGovern), 65
Tresselt, Alvin, 3
Turn the Next Corner (Alcock), 144–
  146
Two Friends, The (Mannheim), 36

Udry, Janice, 151
Umbrella (Yashima), 35, 151

Vestly, Anne-Cath., 138
Viorst, Judith, 5, 71
Vogel, Ilse-Margaret, 40

Waber, Bernard, 39, 63
Wahl, Jan, 77
Warburg, Sandol, 6
Ward, Lynd, 67
Wasson, Valentina, 104
Watson, Jane, 75
Way Mothers Are, The (Schlein), 29
Waybill, Marjorie, 110
Weber, Alfons, 56
Welcome Child (Buck), 109–110
Wersba, Barbara, 34, 65
What Happens When You Go to the
  Hospital (Shay), 58–59

What Would You Do? A Child's Book About Divorce (Cain), 118
What's In the Dark? (Memling), 65
Where Is Daddy? The Story of a Divorce (Goff), 119
Where the Wild Things Are (Sendak), 71–72
While Susie Sleeps (Schneider), 31, 64
Whistle for Willie (Keats), 66
White, E. B., 21
White Snow, Bright Snow (Tresselt), 3
Wiese, Kurt, 66, 67
Will I Have a Friend? (Cohen), 35–36, 96

Winter Noisy Book, The (Brown), 65
Wolde, Gunilla, 75, 90
Wright, Dare, 70

Yashima, Taro, 35, 67, 70, 151
Youngest One (Yashima), 70

"Zachary's Divorce" (Sitea), 124
Zim, Herbert, S., 18, 19
Zindel, Paul, 143
Zion, Gene, 67
Zolotow, Charlotte, 16, 31, 34, 64, 96, 98, 125, 140, 149

General Index

This Index contains topical citations, and lists authors and titles of books in two categories: reference works, and juvenile reading matter not included in the Index of Juvenile Book Authors and Titles.

Abandonment, fear of, 29, 115, 119–120
About Dying (Stein), 19–20
Across the Meadow (Shecter), 8
Adoption, 100–114
  animal allegories about, 112
  "chosen-baby" theme, 104
  court proceedings of, 113
  foster care, 108
  guides for parents about, 100–102
  informing children of, 102–105, 109–110
  play therapy, 111–112
  practical and emotional issues about, 105–106
  psychological vs. biological parenting, 100
  research studies about, 102–103
  sex and reproduction information, 107
  single parent, 112
  transcultural, 110–111
Adoption Adviser, The (McNamara), 100
Adoption and After (Raymond), 100
Amy Loves Goodbyes (Gordon), 45
Anthony, E. J., 114
Anthony, J., 86

Baby sitters
  separation from, 140
  staying with, 39
Bedtime stories, 29–33
Benet, Mary, 102
Berger, A. S., 26
Bergman, Thesi, 52
Beyond the Best Interests of the Child (Goldstein et al.), 100
Bowlby, John, 2, 26, 63, 102
Boy, a Dog, a Frog and a Friend, A (Mayer), 7–8

Caplan, Gerald, 135
Children: A Personal Record for the Use of Adoptive Parents (de Hartog), 110
Chukovsky, K., 99
Church, J., 87

de Hartog, Jan, 110
Death, 1–22
  ambivalence to, 2
  of a child, 20–21
  concepts to help children grasp, 22
  dealing with through life-cycle stories, 3
  denial of, 2

of elderly, 9–16
explanation of, 17–20
of a grandparent, 9–16
grief-work, 2
"mourning at a distance," 21
of a parent, 16–17
of pets and objects, 3–8
questions for discussion, 14
threat of, 20–21
Dentist, visit to, 74–78
Despert, J. L., 115
Divorce, 114–126
books on, 116–126
emotional effects of, 114–115
parental visits, 121–124
reconciliation fantasies, 119–120
statistics on, 114
substitute relationships in, 121
therapy and counseling, 115
Doctor, visit to, 74–78
Dombro, R. H., 51
Dreams and dreaming, 33–34
Dywasuk, C., 100

Edie Changes Her Mind (Johnston)
45–46
Erikson, Erik H., 13
Esselstyn, T. C., 142

Family constellation, changes in, 139–
142
Family-life stories, 107–108, 111, 126,
143
Fanshel, D., 103
Fiction and the Unconscious (Lesser), 1
Financial stress, 136–138
Fire, stress produced by, 148
Flood, stress produced by, 149
Freud, Anna, 27, 51, 52, 78, 87, 100,
105, 122, 146, 147
Friedman, S., 142
Furman, R. A., 2, 26

Garn, Bernard, 74
Geist, Harold, 52
Goldstein, Joseph, 100, 105, 122, 146,
147
Goodenough, E. W., 26
Gordon, Selma, 45
Grandparents
death of, 9–16
relationship in household, 139–140
Grollman, Earl, 2, 17–19, 115, 117, 118
Gross, D. W., 26
Gruber, Ruth, 112

Haller, J. A., 51
Handicapped child, 113
Hass, Alan, 109

Homan, W. E., 87
Hospitalization. *See also* Surgery
anxiety about night sounds, 65
books about, 52–62
emotional effects of, 51–52
independence and autonomy during,
67–68, 70, 71
medical procedures during, 56, 61
of a parent, 11, 142
parents' presence during, 63–64
playacting therapy, 55–56
questions to generate discussion, 53,
55, 67, 69
verbalization of feelings, 68–73
Humphrey, M. E., 102
Hurricanes, stress produced by, 149

Illness and pain, 78. *See also* Hospitalization
Imprisonment of a parent, 142–148
counseling, 147
effects of, 142–143
explanation of, 142–143
prison policy, 146–147
Interracial families, 113

Jaffee, B., 103
Janis, I. L., 86
Jersild, A., 87
Johnston, Johanna, 45

Kadushin, A., 102
Kelly, J., 121
Kessler, J. W., 26
Kimmel, E. A., 27
Kliman, Gilbert, 2, 21, 52, 68, 86, 93,
95, 140, 143
Koupernik, C., 86
Kübler-Ross, Elisabeth, 20

Lanes, S. G., 1
Lasker, Joe, 111
Lesser, Simon, 1, 18, 60, 73, 152
Lewis, M., 86
Lifton, Robert Jay, 102
*Little School at Cottonwood Corners,
The* (Schick), 45

McNamara, Joan, 100, 111
McWhinnie, A. M., 103
Margolies, Marjorie, 112
Mayer, Marianna, 7
Mayer, Mercer, 7
Meathenia, P. S., 27
Michaels, Ruth, 104, 105
Moving to a new home, 93–100
to new country, 97
parents' support during, 95–96
potential stress of, 93–95

Moving to a new home (*cont.*)
 from rural to urban setting, 97
 "transitional objects," 95
 unrealistic books about, 99–100
 when a friend moves, 98
Murray, A., 100
My Journey Home (Partridge), 110–111

Nagera, H., 2, 31
Neilson, J., 108
New Dimensions in Adoption (Randell), 100
Nighttime fears and fantasies, 29–33
 in hospital, 64–65

Opel, Joanne, 111
Oremland, E. K., 52
Oremland, J. D., 52

Palmer, Richard, 146
Parents' working arrangements, change in, 138–139
Parkes, M., 2
Partridge, Jackie, 110
Petrillo, M., 52
Pine, F., 27
Plank, Emma, 52, 61
Playacting therapy
 for adoption, 111–112
 for hospitalization, 55–56
Politics of Adoption, The (Benet), 102
Pringle, M. L. K., 102
Prugh, D. G., 51

Raymond, L., 100
Robertson, J., 51, 63
Rondell, Florence R., 100, 104, 105

Sack, W. H., 142, 143
Sanger, S., 52
Schechter, M. D., 102
Schecter, Ben, 8
Schick, Eleanor, 45
School experiences
 gradual separation from parent, 46–47
 separation fears, 26–27, 34–39
 unsound books about, 45
Schowalter, John E., 2, 20
Seglow, J., 102
Seidler, J., 142
Senn, M., 86
Separation experiences. *See also* Divorce
 from babysitter, 140
 early fear of, 26
 fear of accidental separation, 40–42
 from friend or teacher, 42–43
 in hospital, 62–64

from imprisoned parent, 142–148
 nighttime, 29–33
 nursery school children, 27, 34–39
 overnight visits, 39–40
 from parents, 39–42
 from pet, 44
 types of, 27–28
 unsound books about, 45–46
Sex education, 107
Shore, M., 51
Siblings
 questions to encourage discussion, 92–93
 reactions to birth of, 93
Single-parent families, 112, 124–125, 142, 143
Solnit, Albert J., 20, 86, 100, 105, 122, 146, 147
Speers, R. W., 27
Spitz, R. A., 51
Stein, Sara Bonnett, 19
Stone, L. J., 87
Storms, stress produced by, 149–151
Stress-producing events, 86, 135–136
Surgery. *See also* Hospitalization
 books about, 61–62
 emotional reactions to, 54
 eye, 60
 tonsillectomy, 58–60
Switzer, R. E., 95

Talbert, J. L., 51
Talking About Death (Grollman), 17–19
Talking About Divorce: A Dialogue Between Parent and Child (Grollman), 117–118
They Came To Stay (Margolies), 112
Thomas, S., 142
Tooley, K., 93–94
Toys
 bedtime, 32
 in hospital, 52

Veil, C., 138
Vernick, J., 20
Visit to the Dentist, A (Garn), 74

Wallerstein, J., 121
Webster, J., 27
Wedge, P., 102
Wessel, Morris A., 16
Wolfenstein, Martha, 7, 21, 87
Wolff, Sula, 68, 86, 103, 136
Working with Children in Hospitals (Plank), 61

You and Your Child: A Guide for Adoptive Parents (Rondell), 105

9 780595 167203